WHEN CARING IS NOT ENOUGH

Resolving Conflicts Through Fair Fighting

David Augsburger

Regal Books
A Division of GL Publications
Ventura, CA U.S.A.

Other books in the "Caring Enough" series:
Caring Enough to Confront
Caring Enough to Forgive/to Not Forgive
Caring Enough to Hear and Be Heard

The foreign language publishing of all Regal books is under the direction of GLINT. GLINT provides financial and technical help for the adaptation, translation, and publishing of books for millions of people worldwide. For information regarding translation contact: GLINT, P.O. Box 6688, Ventura, California 93006.

For the sake of easier reading, the use of the pronouns, *he, him* and *his* in this publication refer for the most part to both male and female in the generic sense.

Published by Regal Books
A Division of GL Publications
Ventura, California 93006
Printed in U.S.A.

Library of Congress Cataloging in Publication data

Augsburger, David W.
When caring is not enough.

("Caring enough" series)
Bibliography: p.
1. Interpersonal relations. 2. Social conflict.
3. Social skills. 4. Fairness. 5. Social justice.
I. Title. II. Series.
HM132.A93 1983 158'.2 83-9577
ISBN 0-8307-0884-7

To Nancy

Once a complement
Who saw
Valued
Called for equality

Often a symmetrical opponent
Who met
Engaged
Fought for mutuality

Joyfully a parallel partner
Who invites and
Excites my growth as
Co-discoverer of
What can be done
When Caring Is Not Enough.

WHEN CARING IS NOT ENOUGH
SKILLS FOR FAIR FIGHTING

Introduction

Read Instructions Before Experimentation

The skills, strategies, and insights in this fair-fighting manual are for personal use only. Application to a friend, spouse, parent, or child is contraindicated (no good at all). Any attempt to prescribe for another is effective only in intensifying the previously unsuccessful conflict patterns or in producing even worse modes of unfair fighting. (No help at all.)

When utilized for personal rather than interpersonal power, these methods of ending self-defeating patterns and beginning alternate ways of working jointly at problem solving can lead to mutually satisfactory solutions.

Discover your own inner instructions before experimenting with change. We learn, trust, and perpetuate our patterns of dodging or dealing with conflict by instructing ourselves with inner statements which warn or urge us on even in repeating self-defeating behaviors.

Hearing, clarifying, and often contradicting these self-instructions that we use in place of thinking can reveal how powerless they are and free us to explore new thoughts, write new inner instructions, and live with new freedom.

The opening and concluding chapters—prologue and epilogue—can be read as a basic introduction to fair fighting in personal relationships with particular application for marital conflict. Although the final chapter will be most useful after exploring the thirty ways of working toward mutuality and equality, if you prefer the vertical styles of someone-must-be-in-charge, then turn to it as soon as you find yourself disagreeing with the equal-horizontal focus on just relationships.

Whether used privately, or in a dyadic relationship with friend or spouse, or as a discussion starter in a small group, the thirty days of experimentation can provide resources for growth and self-discovery. Any success in identifying and writing out your own self-instructions on any or all of these conflict options will be rewarding. The most lasting means of changing our automatic defensive or coping behaviors is to set rumors afloat in the unconscious that better ways are possible. To instruct the self with new inner dialogues sets free hopes of change and growth. Explore the ways you instruct yourself, even on those areas where you now feel confident.

There are other ways waiting within your own creativity. Change is difficult for those who believe it so, it comes slowly and surely for those who claim the freedom to make purposeful change. The most lasting growth takes place in smaller steps, chosen purposefully from within.

Thirty days of change can set new instructions, new intentions loose within the soul. It is a kind of growth called *repentance.* It is worth the effort and the cost to learn ways of working through differences with equal regard in a search for equal justice.

David Augsburger
January, 1983
Goshen, Indiana

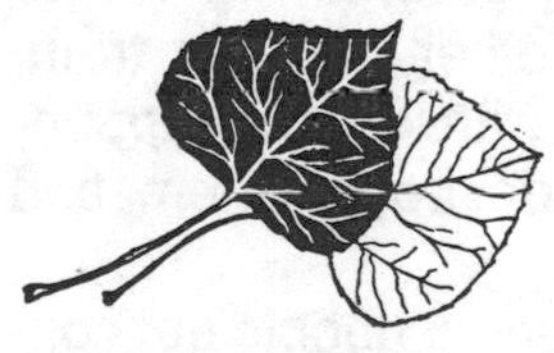

Prologue
Fair Fighting

"All things are possible if you care enough. Painful differences are erased, conflict is resolved, anger dissipates, things fall into place."

Caring is not enough.

In the name of caring, persons can confidently take over and live others' lives for them with a conscience that is not only clear, it is rewarding them for "caring."

In the guise of caring, those with the divine right to rule can direct, shape, mold their world into their own image, and sleep peacefully believing in a good will that they were "caring."

In the practice of caring, parents can absorb their children into their own unfinished dramas, assign them roles, tasks, life scripts that will fulfill their own sense of unlived life, and do it compassionately as "caring."

In the politics of caring, males have taken care of females with a dominance which varied from benevolent generosity to malevolent exploitation, and have felt the divine right of hierarchical "caring."

In the pretext of simply caring, spouses have engulfed partners, incorporated them into their own careers, life-styles, dreams, and invited fatal dependencies while calling it "caring."

In the presumption of caring, parents may lie to kids, partners may protect each other from the truth, whole families may avoid dealing with what is happening by denying the obvious that is destroying them, and justify it as "caring."

In the good intentions called caring, people get controlled, manipulated, cajoled, coerced, used, and abused.

Caring is not enough. There must be something more, something guaranteeing a more mutually satisfactory, jointly chosen, equally beneficial outcome.

The something more is *justice.*

The cry for justice begins in early childhood when fairness and equality become important in play, work, rewards, and punishments.

But wanting justice and getting justice can be two very different things. The behaviors which press for fairness are often sharply criticized or not permitted. We learn early to settle for less than justice without speaking up.

The Right to Fight

"I am fed up with your idea of fairness. It's always two for you and none for me. But what can I say? Your view is 'to each according to his production,' my view is 'to each according to need.' What shall I do?"

When justice is seen in very different ways, then

those differences must be worked through. When opportunities for fair distribution are blocked, then the obstacles must be worked out.

The right to fight is a foundational layer in human personhood connected to the freedom to love. Both can be creative, fulfilling drives within humans and communities. Both can be destructive. Caring that consumes, or conflict that destroys, are evils which must be interrupted. Caring that frees, and conflict that reconstructs a relationship, more justly excites new life and invites deeper trust.

Among the rights learned in early childhood, the right to remain silent in the face of injustice, and the right to overlook differences in order to avoid conflict or evade confrontation are among the most common defenses.

When the instruction is centered in ways of suppressing conflict and of not expressing feelings of injustice, then the behaviors learned are largely negative, defensive, and reactive. When these get overloaded, the conflict which erupts is overcharged with irritation, overwhelmed with feelings of helplessness and hopelessness, and the fighting which follows is desperate, survival-oriented, and dirty in style. When one has internalized the right to fight for both intimacy and integrity, one can learn to fight rightly.

Fighting Rightly

"I'm embarrassed that I resent your self-confidence so deeply. I should be able to overlook it, but I feel so taken for granted. I've no right to complain or to ask for change, but I'd like to."

The right to fight precedes learning how to fight rightly. As long as strong internal prohibitions inhibit conflict and postpone negotiation until the limits of

Right Relationships Honor Rights Within Relationship

I. You have the right to act toward others according to your own beliefs and values (not according to theirs), to live your own life (not be lived by others), to live out your own decisions and to live with their consequences.

II. You have the right to see others as equal (regardless of how they see you), to esteem others as neither superior nor inferior (in spite of how they esteem you).

III. You have the right to renegotiate relationships (although the other resist review), to take new positions (though the other prefers the old), to change your mind (even when another doubts you have one).

IV. You have the right to fail (therefore the right to choose freely), the right to make mistakes (therefore the right to take risks).

V. You have the right to see your own perceptions, to feel your own feelings, to think your own thoughts, to act your own actions, to experience your own accountability.

endurance are reached, then the hassle that results will bring out the worst.

When unapproved and therefore unpracticed fight patterns emerge, they tend to be one-way, win-lose, all-or-nothing strategies that wreak havoc on the relationship. Dirty fighting is the curse of habitual non-fighting. When families, couples, associates, fellow workers have many little fights, they are much less likely to accumulate feelings until a large explosion erupts. Where there is fair, more immediate and mutually satisfactory negotiation practiced, the urge to fight in controlling or manipulative ways dwindles away. But this assumes one has claimed and accepted the right to fight as necessary.

For many persons, the right to resist imposition from others has been surrendered. This comes not only from the training to be selfless and nice—offered in childhood, but also from the adult piety which sees mature Christian faith as giving up all "rights." "The real Christian, like the Master, has no rights, so there is nothing to defend; no demands, so there is nothing to be angry about; no ambitions, so there is nothing to be jealous about; he or she is already dead, so no one can hurt him, no one can kill her." This too easy resignation of one's values has a doubly tragic impact: it acquiesces to evil done to the self, it models such passivity as true maturity for others.

A relationship is as healthy as its understandings are just, fair, and trustworthy; to yield these without effort in the name of unselfishness is to work for injustice. To surrender in the name of love without resisting evil is to destroy the integrity of human connectedness which keeps love alive.

Right relationships honor the rights within relationship. "Acting toward others as you would have them act toward you," as the golden rule of community commands, takes one's own assessment of justice as the criteria for service to the neighbor. To do unto others whatever is required of you is no service to either self or other, it is slavish subservience. Along with the right to do as you would have done to you are the other rights of seeing the other in equal regard; claiming the right to change, grow, and repent; owning the privilege of being one's own responsible self; and accepting the privilege of risking and failing. All these follow from the rule of responsible self-chosen justice.

Right relationships are built from a balance of love and justice. Love is the valuing of the neighbor, justice is the arithmetic of love that distributes the caring and support with equal regard. Love and justice are both indispensable. Neither is enough alone. We must go on offering caring. We must continue struggling for justice. The struggle and the embrace are the basic movements of human relationship. Caring guarantees the understanding and prizing, justice protects the integrity and balance between persons.

Fighting Jointly

"I am angry at what is going wrong between us, but the anger is directed at you, not at the problems in our relationship. If I dealt with the way we get into these blaming cycles, we might make some progress, but at the moment I'm turning all my blaming toward you. So what's new?"

Conflict that is focused on the relationship rather than on putting down the self or attacking the other has the best chance of maintaining clear goals and clean means.

Attacking the other person, whether done subtly or straightforwardly, increases the tension, accelerates

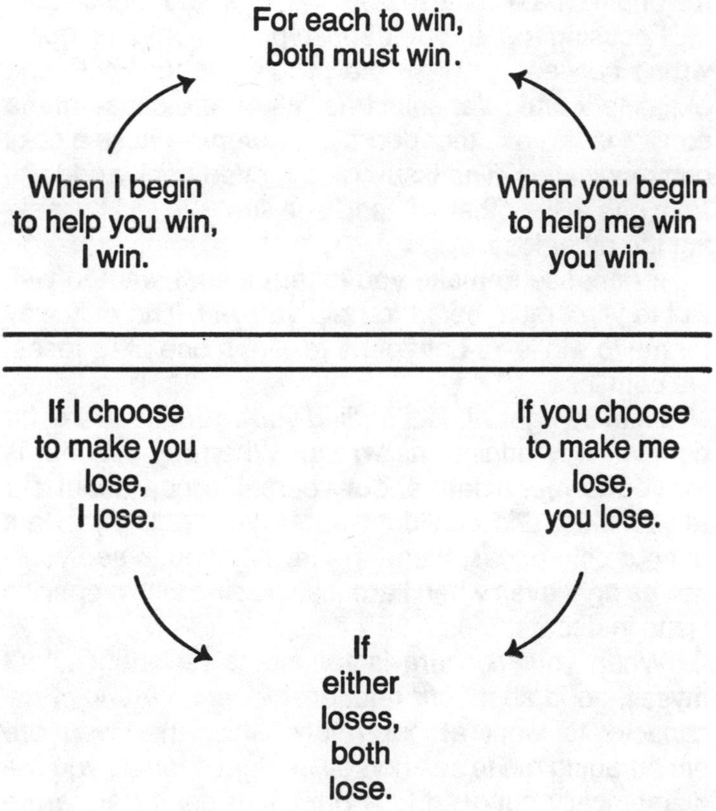

For each to win,
both must win.

When I begin
to help you win,
I win.

When you begin
to help me win
you win.

If I choose
to make you
lose,
I lose.

If you choose
to make me
lose,
you lose.

If
either
loses,
both
lose.

Diagram 1

the arousal, widens the distance between the participants, creates an either-or situation of shifting blame. It adds injury to injury so one must recover not only from the original pain but also from the attempted resolution.

Focusing on the relationship, on what is going wrong between us, lays the problem where both can examine it and offer solutions. When the cause of the conflict is laid at either doorstep, defensiveness blocks communication. The issue gets moved back and forth from one to the other as each one seeks to win by making the other lose.

If I choose to make you lose, I lose. I want to win. But to win I must begin to help you win. The only way for me to win is for both of us to win. If one of us loses, we both lose.

I can be right without finding you wrong. You can be right without judging me wrong. When my concern is for you to feel alright about yourself, good about our relationship, and confident about your ability to work out our differences, then I am inviting you to see yourself as right even when I am disagreeing with a specific issue in debate.

When your concern is for me to feel right about myself, good about our relationship, and certain of my capacity to work at our relationship, then you are encouraging me to see myself as right even as you are diametrically opposed to a particular point I am arguing.

We may differ in fact, but not in act.

We may disagree on a problem, but not on the process.

We may fight about the content, but not damage the context. The fight issue does not dictate the fight style. The "what" does not control the "how." What we are negotiating can be separated from how we are going about it. We can deal with most any "what" if we have worked out a trustworthy "how."

What you think, feel, believe, all emerge from how you perceive the world. Out of my history I organize my world view in my own unique way. Out of your history you assemble your world view in your special way. I value my way as valid for me. I respect your way as having integrity for you. I will disagree with what you see without denigrating how you came to see it in that way. You may share your "what" freely. I will join you in finding what's "what" for both of us without putting down how you came to be where you are or apologizing how I arrived at where I am.

Fighting Cleanly

Clean fighting is not a fortuitous combination of compatible personalities, it is an intentional commitment to being there for the other person in both agreeable and disagreeable situations.

Being there has a number of levels of commitment that are foundational, the bottom lines of relationship.

Being there is a commitment to availability without threat of avoidance, distance, flight, retreat, neutrality, superficiality, or termination of the relationship.

Being there is a commitment to responsibility without resorting to blaming, impugning, mind reading, excusing, or any other means of evasion.

Being there is a commitment to flexibility instead of stubbornly holding the line, rigidly refusing any concessions, firmly setting nonnegotiable limits that yield nothing, that demand an all-or-nothing, take-it-or-leave-it conclusion.

Being there is a commitment to specificity without making general complaints, universal statements in absolute language that merely ventilate frustration and

Fighting Cleanly . . .
. . . is BEING THERE with . . .

1. Availability: Effective fighting begins with one or both persons committing themselves to be genuinely present and authentically involved in resolving the conflict creatively.

2. Responsibility: Each party accepts full responsibility for the thoughts, feelings, acts, values, and perceptions he or she contributes to the conflict.

3. Flexibility: Each person offers a willingness to make some degree of change, so that both can move toward a joint solution.

4. Specificity: Both persons seek to focus the conflict on real, significant issues that point toward a practical outcome that is within the range of possibility.

5. Clarity: The message intended and the impact received are nearly the same, communication is achieved. For this to happen, the words, tone of voice, facial expression, posture, must all be congruent with each other and with the setting in which they are said.

offer no useful, practical, possible, mutually profitable outcome.

Being there is a commitment to clarity without resorting to deliberately vague, distorted, inconsistent, or incongruent messages.

The choice to clean up fight styles is a commitment to genuine presence. Almost all forms of dirty fighting are ways of moving over, under, away from, out of range, against, in spite of, in place of, rather than standing with the other.

Fighting Fairly

Fighting fairly has a certain rhythm, vigor, and routine about it. More than a routine of responses it is a route traveled together which guarantees safety while working with the threat of rejection, and security while dealing with the request to change.

Unfair fighting has its own routines that are just as predictable and repetitive as are fair patterns of conflict. Frequently this triggers the cumulative frustration as familiar moves and countermoves occur. Thus the absence or presence of a routine is not the sign of fairness, the issue is, Are they confusing or clarifying, bonding or alienating?

All fights are by appointment either consciously and jointly chosen or unconsciously and unilaterally chosen. Those at a mutually acceptable time and place are far more productive.

All fights attempt to focus the issue. Some do it sharply, narrowly, usefully. Others focus on the person, his fears, her weaknesses, his failures, her family. The question is not whether to focus, but whether to do it with creative purpose or competitive instinct.

All fights make demands. The sharp contrast is between the unfair, unlimited, unconditional demands

Fair Fighting

Timing and Turf: (the place)	Fight only by appointment At a mutually acceptable time In a mutually agreeable place. (Pick time and place together.)
Focus and Feedback: (the problem)	Focus the frustration sharply Clarify the issue narrowly, Verify with feedback. (Express the issue cleanly, clearly.)
Request and Response: (the solution)	Make the demand for change. Keep it specific, useful, possible. Accept partial or total agreement. (Invite change in small single steps.)
Review and Reward: (the celebration)	Reflect on the agreement reached. Reschedule further issues for later times. Reward the other for listening and responding. (Celebrate each step of progress and growth.)

of dirty fighting, or the specific, useful, possible demands which are in small increments.

All fights get reviewed and all fighters seek some reassurance that the process was necessary, the results worth the cost. Where the injury inflicted seems greater than the benefits achieved, the review often turns to self-justifications: "At least I was honest about how I felt," although what was offered may have been brutal openness rather than honesty. When the conflict has reached a mutually satisfactory solution, the review leads to rewards and celebration.

The fight route, whether fair or unfair, touches the same bases, but with utterly different results. It is not a question whether to include the steps, but which direction to take with them—away from each other, or toward mutual understanding.

Focusing Sharply

The primary skill to be learned is the art of focusing the complaint or beef clearly and making the request for change as effectively as possible.

Spelling out a complaint requires reflection on just what is going wrong, just what is causing difficulty, and just what change is desired. The self-examination which precedes an effective confrontation should surface the central gripes that are stimulating the differences and boil them down to one narrow demand. Attempting to work through more than one issue at a time, or to process a complex multi-level demand, only leads to frustration on frustration.

It is crucial that the problem be presented clearly and understood as fully as possible before any solutions are requested or offered. Until a mutual understanding is achieved, any attempt at solving it is premature and counterproductive.

Questions for Focusing

1. What is it, really, that is getting to me?
2. What is it, really, that I want to do about it?
3. What are the other options open to me?
4. What alternate ways of seeing, thinking, feeling are there?
5. What are the risks involved, the issues at stake?
6. What is the worst that could result from pressing the point?
7. What realistically do I really need, not just want?
8. How important is this change to me?
9. How difficult would this change be for the other?
10. How can I present my case so it can't be misunderstood?

Presenting the issue clearly with impact as well as with appeal is not just a gift fair fighters have or don't have. It is a discipline. The willingness to cross-examine one's own inner prosecutor until the case is well prepared saves a lot of emotional wear and tear on both parties.

When the issue has been spelled out in specific behaviors, their actual effects and the resulting feelings, it can hardly be misunderstood.

The simplest formula is to report, (1) What you do is . . . , (2) What it does to me is . . . , (3) What I feel is . . . . This spells out the action, its impact and my feelings. All three elements are needed for understanding the problem.[1]

For example: "When you come home an hour late in the evening without a call, it completely disrupts the dinner hour for us all, and I feel angry and mistrustful of your other promises."

Or, "When you criticize me in front of others, it touches something very painful for me since I was shamed frequently as a kid, and I feel like hiding."

Or, "When you stress making sales more than providing service to the customers I feel pressure to persuade or push people to buy, and I feel unhappy with my work."

Or, "When you drive so fast on ice I get uptight because it is not just your life being threatened, it's mine and I feel angry."

Requesting Clearly

The three parts—the action, its impact, and my feelings—help in understanding the problem between us. When the issue can be expressed in mutually interchangeable words—that is, each could describe the situation in similar words as the other uses, then it is possible to move to the third step of making the *request* for change and receiving the *response.* We change best in small increments, in specific manageable behaviors. Requesting the rebuilding of large pieces of behavior is much less likely to result in creative change. Appropriate requests for the problems stated above are these:

"I want a phone call as soon as possible after you become aware that you will be more than a half hour late."

"I am open to hear your criticism in private. Just ask for a time and place and I will be available."

"I want to be equally as concerned for the welfare of the customer as for the success of sales. I would like to hear you stress both."

"I want to do the driving when roads are icy, or to be assured that you are easily able to turn or stop."

Specific requests, broken down into discrete parts, fractionated into as small a step as possible, are most likely to be accepted and acted upon.

Rewarding Genuinely

New ways of responding do not last unless they are either so self-rewarding that the person celebrates the change privately or the other person reinforces the movement with warm appreciation and commendation. When the new response is largely the desire of the other person, it will rarely continue unless there is twice as much appreciation expressed as criticism given for slipping back on occasion. The ratio of rewards to reminders is so crucial that to be effective it most frequently must be rewards, "10," reminders, "0." Trusting the other person's ability to change is best demonstrated by affirming the positive movements and living with the slowness to change old automatic or habitual responses that is our human pattern.

Since for many persons, a residual level of guilt remains after any conflict no matter how fairly fought, the rewards and celebration offer inner reinforcement, reassurance, and rewards to your own self as well as the other. Celebration of the end of a successful negotiation is beneficial both ways. What is a gift to the other is also a gift to oneself.

Internalizing Learning

New learnings, new experiences, new ways of thinking, feeling, responding, negotiating, and rewarding must all be internalized until they become natural, authentic choices which emerge from within. This process is not a mysterious or magical reconstruction of the unconscious, it is a deliberate, conscious choice to change the inner conversation which goes on in our thinking, feeling, planning states.

We use language to formulate plans of action and to guide our behaviors. It is a sort of internal dialogue we carry on with ourselves in preparation for a confrontation, in the midst of a conflict, and afterward.

The simplest such conversations begin at the morning mirror when self-image is reflected more clearly than facial image,

"Look at your self, see how you look?"

"Yea, pretty terrible."

"Boy, are you right. You're overweight too."

"Well, I could lose a few pounds."

"A few? Well, it wouldn't matter if that were your only problem."

"You mean . . ."

"I don't have to tell you how badly you blew it yesterday . . ."

Our self-concept is based in part on the ratio of

Self Instructions Checklist

Old Self Instructions	**New Self Instructions**
	Preparation
"I just know the other guy will be testy, nasty, or pushy."	"I can be firm without being irritable or blunt."
"I'll get so frustrated I'm likely to lose my cool and blow my top."	"I know what I want to do so I can manage the emotions."
"I'm so fed up I can't hold this in much longer."	"Three deep breaths and I'll be relaxed no matter what he says or does."
"One more dig and I'll give him what he's asking for."	"This could get a bit tense but I can stay with the task and negotiate my goals."
	Excitation
"Oh-oh. I'm getting really bugged. He's not going to get away with pushing me around."	"I'm feeling warm in the face, my muscles are getting tight. I'm more aroused than I knew."
"I'm so tight inside I'm going to explode and get it off my chest."	"It's reasonable to get annoyed, but my real concern is to get things clear between us."
"Boy am I furious. How dare you treat me like this, you . . . "	"I really do care how this comes out. I'll take time to talk to myself so I'll not flip out."

Confrontation

"You're all negatives, you insensitive clod. All you can offer is criticism."	"I'll look for positives and potential agreements without assuming the worst."
"Obviously you're out to get me so why shouldn't I give you a bit of the same . . ."	"As long as I keep my cool, I'm in control of my half of the confrontation."
"If I don't stand up for me . . ."	"I don't need to prove myself."

Reward

"Well, at least I was honest about how I felt."	"I did it. I kept my cool and focused on the issue."

negative to positive things we say about ourselves in such internal conversations. The statements we make to ourselves about ourselves can trigger a wide range of reactions: anxiety, shame, guilt, envy, anger, resentment, and low self-esteem.[2]

The self instructions we use to warn ourselves against the worst or discourage ourselves from seeking the best are the key to inviting change within. These self instructions are frequently recorded announcements from our family of origin. If one listens closely, the inflections of parents and grandparents can be clearly heard. Along with these voices from the past instructing us on how to think, feel, and act are the recorded pronouncements of our own early learnings. The conflict behaviors of childhood, youth, and young adulthood remain with us in the warnings we repeat within, the guidelines we lay down as anxiety rises.

Tracking down the internal self statements made, and replacing the negative ones with more positive, more effective self instructions is a process of teasing out the tangled thoughts and rewriting the self-defeating sentences. Examining your own repertoire of positive and negative comments—learned or inherited, setting new alternatives afloat in the unconscious, and keeping new instructions aware in the conscious all work together in building new conflict behaviors.

Looking at the two sets of internal instructions given in the checklist, you can write out a set of inner dialogues heard as you approach, engage, or review your interactions. Note the self-fulfilling prophesies of failure. Guess which fears about the other tend to be fulfilled by the bad chemistry partially caused by your predictions. Then replace the old instructions with new. In learning anger management, carrying the new statements on a card and reviewing them, before a confrontation is initiated, produces the rapid and radical change. As the internal dialogue replaces panic with calm, suspicion with trust, insecurity with confidence, evaluation with understanding, feeling manipulated with self-understanding, diffused frustration with clear goals, then the external behavior changes with the internal instructions.

In the following series of experiences, the old self instructions on thirty dirty conflict patterns will be charted (although yours may be more colorful or creative) and a clean set of mutual, equal, effective instructions will be suggested. Write your own. Learn them well. Set them loose within.

When Caring Is Not Enough

A Thirty-Day Experiment

Thirty ways to fight dirty or clean.

The following collection of strategies for fair or foul fighting is not exhaustive, but is suggestive of the many ways of either destroying or creating effective relationship.

They may be read consecutively to understand others, or discussed individually with a small group, a marriage partner, a friend.

The self instructions offer a structure for exploring the inner self statements used to direct, or select behaviors in times of conflict. Old instructions can be revised or completely replaced with new, more useful inner guidelines.

As guidelines for changing others' behavior, these materials will fail, as have most other strategies for altering another. As steps to greater freedom and growth in oneself, they are limited only by your willingness to become more aware.

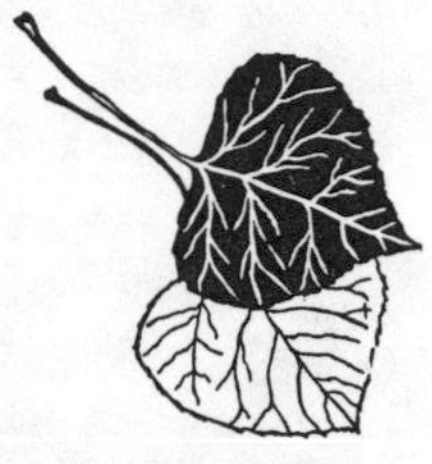

Day One
Timing

Old Self Instructions

Catch them off guard

Start the argument
when least expected.
Drop the criticism
when she's
unprepared.
Raise the issue
when he's overloaded.
Spring the fight
when she's
overwhelmed.
Choose the time
that is best for you.

New Self Instructions

Take time to set a time

I want
Equal willingness,
Equal readiness,
Equal openness,
At a mutually chosen,
Mutually satisfactory
time.

"By the way, may I have a word?"
(sounds incidental, but isn't)

"I know you're busy but this will only take a minute."
(sounds innocent, but isn't)

"I've a comment on the way you handled ______."
(sounds trivial, but time will tell)

If you want to have it your way, take them by surprise.

A fight is often over before it begins, the outcome may be fixed from the outset. One-way-winners fight on their own schedule (when the other is off balance), at their own initiative (when the other is least prepared), to their own advantage (when they are up, steamed, demanding control).

Timing can serve many purposes whether one is aware of its function or simply acts habitually. Coercive timing rushes the other, pushes the other, reduces the other's freedom to respond fully and fairly. Manipulative timing catches the other at a point of psychological weakness, physical fatigue, or shaky self-esteem. Avoidant timing postpones, evades, eludes a desired conversation in hope it will go away. Haphazard timing that springs a criticism in the midst of celebration, concentration, or distraction can be crazy-making.

If one's hope is to rework the other, then the surprise attack may have its desired coercive or manipulative effect. If one hopes to work through a difference, then an agreed time with a known agenda brings the most positive results.

Fight only by appointment.

All fights are by appointment, of course, either of conscious choice or of unconscious intuition.

The time may be set deliberately at a moment of optimal readiness for both, or it can be allowed to just happen by impulse, at a time that is to one's own advantage.

Since a good beginning is often half the fight, the self instructions used to guide its initiation frequently determine its emotional tone, the positions which will be taken, the outcomes which will be reached. Such instructions are:

Pick a time when you are at your best, the other at the worst. If pressures, stress, schedule, fatigue put the other in a bind, he or she will have to listen.

Don't choose the time, let it choose you. If you trust the timing to happenstance, you are then beyond responsibility. "It just came up because of what you said. I'd never have given it a second thought."

Don't negotiate a time, wait for an opening, an opportune moment, a pause when it "feels right" to you. Entrusting a crucial decision to the impulses of irritation, impatience, or anger is delegating a central concern to the automatic processes of self-defense, or the inner balancing of emotional ledgers, or the instincts of survival.

Don't jointly set a time, instead seize the initiative, claim the moment, state your case whether the other is prepared to hear it or not. The best defense is a strong offense.

Consciously or unconsciously, people favor the time which favors them. Morning people prefer getting things out at the beginning of the day; evening people are inclined to work things through at the day's end. And there are those who prefer any time that is time out for the other.

Mutually favored times, though seemingly hard to find, emerge as people negotiate trusted patterns for resolving differences. As jointly acceptable times are found, appointments made and kept, agenda expressed and dealt with, people create safe pathways along which conflicts can move toward resolution. As pathways become familiar, trustworthy, and satisfying, then one can tolerate waiting for the agreed appointment.

Dirty Fighting Code

"My time is the right time. I just say it when I feel like it. I'll talk about it when I'm good and ready. You think this is a bad time, just be grateful I didn't bring it up when I was lying awake at 3:00 A.M."

Fair Fighting Creed

"I'll check out whether this is an acceptable time to work on differences. I will not surprise, ambush, or decide alone on the appropriate time. I will ask for and I will keep appointments for working through frustrations."

Exercises

Reflect on your three most recent conflicts.

1. Did you schedule the confrontation?
2. Was it an individual or joint decision?

Plan a conversation on a significant difference.

1. Rehearse your request for a mutually agreed time.
2. Plan a clear statement of the agenda that presents the issue in a neutral yet open way.

Day Two
Turf

Old Self Instructions

Pick your best turf

Spring the fight
where you are
comfortable.
Slip the criticism
in front of kids or
guests.
Drop the bombshell
just as you're leaving.
Pick the turf
where you feel secure
and the other insecure.

New Self Instructions

Choose neutral turf

I want
Equal comfort,
Equal security,
Equal freedom,
In a mutually,
Satisfactory place.

"I'm not going to confront him in his office, I'd feel intimidated. I think I'll invite him to lunch."
(choose neutral turf)

"I don't want to make a big thing out of it, I'll just mention it in passing when we're with others."
(choose protected turf)

"She's busy with dinner, I can raise it now without stirring up a big discussion."
(choose emotionally loaded turf)

Whose turf, which turf, and why is it selected as the scene of the conflict will significantly shape the direction it takes.

Emotionally loaded turf confuses the conflict and tends to overload with secondary issues. A fight in a bedroom easily elicits the fears, needs, hurts, and angers surrounding intimacy. These glue to the original complaint and make clear definition and frank negotiation difficult. A kitchen, historically women's turf, is undergoing changes parallel to the redefining of sexual roles in our culture. All the feelings of inequality, unfair distribution of junk work, and unjust role definitions, rise to cloud the air. Any emotionally loaded place will live up to its name.

Protected turf is used not only for hit-and-run conflict styles but by those who feel a great power differential that must be neutralized to manage the fears. Raising an issue in front of children, when with another couple, or while with a spouse's parents can provide situational protection. The anger aroused and repressed is equal to and often double to the amount of protection provided. The cost of "protection" is postponed, but it is usually charged and paid.

Advantageous turf includes any setting largely owned by a person. This personal turf becomes his "castle," or her "fortress." An office, a den, a personal bedroom, a shop, a studio can become an extension of a person or personality. While on one's own turf, with an invited guest, one feels greater security, lower stress. But the reverse can be true when the turf is invaded unannounced or uninvited. To walk into your son's or daughter's room uninvited and confront on a violated curfew is a double assault. Every child deserves his or her own private area or room which is free from invasion and criticism.

Neutral turf is the best place for effective resolution of differences. Most persons have areas which are off limits for conflict; for couples, the bedroom is best reserved for rest and intimacy. Conflicts can be taken to the family room for negotiation or worked out across the table.

Many couples find the optimal setting is a walk in the open air. The muscles are moving to burn off the surplus arousal; the neutrality of the sidewalk, the freedom to not maintain eye contact—which can be controlling, the recognition that this walk has a beginning and a necessary completion, all invite responsible working through.

For some persons a public place is more neutral. For others a car provides privacy, appropriate closeness; but it is better parked during a confrontation than negotiating traffic while negating each other.

The needs for personal space—distance from an antagonist—varies from person to person. A frequently used exercise for marital partners is to stand them nose to nose, then ask each to back up to the appropriate distance for disagreement, then compare the space needed. Where the average person chooses an arm's length distance, there are those who prefer six inches, and others who demand the proverbial ten-foot pole. Two seminarians, with high inhibition of conflict, discovered in counseling that their conflict needs of wide space—each needed at least twelve feet—had made all conflict impossible in their first year in a two-room efficiency apartment. The eight-foot rooms or their car were the only available spaces. They chose to use the empty chapel, as long as neither claimed the pulpit.

Choose a neutral turf, a mutually agreeable setting, so that each experiences equal comfort, security, and freedom to work through the mixed feelings and contrasting perspectives that create conflict.

Dirty Fighting Code

"I need all the help, all the advantage, all the edge I can get. If my moving in on another intimidates him a bit, I will invade his space, stand over him and use the situation, the bystanders, the obvious discomfort, to press for my advantage."

Fair Fighting Creed

"Anything that reduces comfort, threatens security, inhibits freedom for either or both of us in a conflict works against what we hope to achieve. I will work for a mutually satisfactory setting, a common neutral turf."

Exercises

For recognition of your own patterns . . .

1. Check out the distance you need in order to feel unthreatened or uninvaded during a conflict. Does it vary when with people you see as more powerful? Less powerful?
2. Make a list of neutral settings for conflict resolu-

tion with your spouse, child, sibling, co-worker, or friend. Discuss these with the other person to see if you have any of these in common.

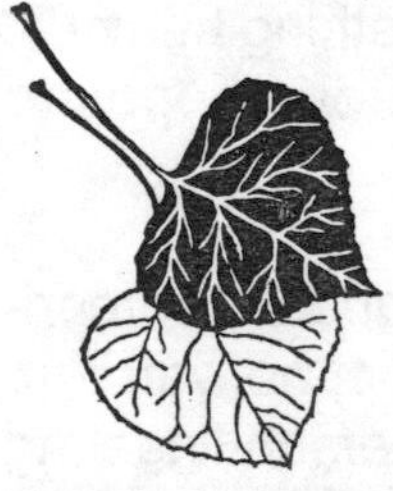

Day Three
Atmosphere

Old Self Instructions

Step up the anxiety

Sulk to set the stage.
Stall to build tension.
Salt with sarcasm.
Escape with busyness.
Top with hysteric overreaction.
Load with foreboding overcontrol.

New Self Instructions

Set a caring atmosphere

I want . . .
Equal relaxation,
Equal genuineness,
Equal control,
Equal caring,
With mutual trust for each other.

"I can tell a storm is gathering from the feel of the air. It's like the calm before everything breaks loose."
(silence is violence too, you know)

"I hate conflict. I withdraw into silence when I feel it coming, hoping it will go away."
(sulking to avoid conflict is like stealing to promote honesty)

"Nothing gets to me like black looks, short answers, grim, glum attitudes. When somebody gives me the sullen treatment I brace myself for something heavy."
(stepping up the anxiety fuels the fire one hopes to quench)

A conflict tends to create an atmosphere appropriate to its own nature. For a blaming battle, no warm-up is necessary, all that is needed is one person fingering the foe, another groveling. But for a negative personality, behavior, or schedule hassle, a sullen, silent, resentful period sets the stage by warming up old resentments, provoking fresh fears. Or for a prolonged cold war, silent withdrawal, deliberate distance, cool treatment is the preferred climate.

What people are afraid to talk out, they act out. The fears that block an open approach to an emerging confrontation get expressed in stiffened posture, broken eye contact, tightened gesture, increased distance, scheduled avoidance.

The self instructions that lie behind the backing away from relationship are gifts from the conflict shyness of our own childhood and the unfinished immaturities of our families of origin.

Inner instruction 1: *Sulk to set the stage.* The other will ignore you, outthink you, dismiss you lightly unless you impress him/her with how deeply you are hurt, how grievously you have been injured, how gravely you feel misused. When the seriousness of the situation has been established, the proper atmosphere is created in which it is clear that you are the hurtee and the other the hurter.

Inner instruction 2: *Stall to build tension.* Refuse to respond to the first query on what's wrong. Deny, evade, belittle the situation in words while showing greater sadness in tone and demeanor. By all means let the conflict ripen. Time is on the complaintant's side. As the suffering extends, the guilt builds.

Inner instruction 3: *Salt with sarcasm.* A few understated words have provocative power at this stage. "Obviously you care about what's going on . . . " A well chosen line can imply whole paragraphs and soften up the other before any real words begin.

Inner instruction 4: *Escape with busyness.* Extending the prefight anxiety arousal by being understandably unavailable, doubling the activities, fulfilling obligations will all serve to postpone the conversation until the situation is more to your advantage.

If none of these produce the desired results of bringing the other person around to your way of thinking without an open confrontation or stimulating anxiety, guilt, insecurity, then one can top it off with exaggerated overreaction (if you have a natural tendency toward mood swings) or load the situation with foreboding overcontrol (if your personality tends to be level and emotionally restrained).

Such inner orders are the stuff of which self-fulfilling prophecies are made. Self-defeating prophecies arise from accelerated anxiety, escalated resentments, inflated fears. These combine to create the cyclical hassles which they were intended to avoid. The very strategies we design to elude conflict evoke it. The only way away from the authentic differences in a relationship is to find a way through those disagreements.

Effective negotiation rises not from upping the ante of anxiety, but from affirming a floor of confidence, a basis of relaxation with each other, an affirmation of equal control, supported by a genuine caring for the fulfillment and satisfaction of both. Clear statements that express what one hopes, fears, or desires of the other build the mutual trust that is the foundation of real dialogue.

Dirty Fighting Code

"Better to suffer silently until the other presses for resolution, then I'm in control since s/he is wondering what is wrong, what s/he has done. When they have hurt enough they come crawling."

Fair Fighting Creed

"My objections, irritations, or demands are my concerns. They are mine to own, mine to share, mine to resolve with the other. I will report them directly, as immediately as appropriate, as negotiable concerns."

Exercises

1. List your favorite passive-aggressive strategies used to soften up the other person's position or attitude without direct conversation—stalling, sulking, sarcasm, busyness, neutrality, avoidance, postponement, etc., etc.
2. Note the pros and cons you feel about (1) past attempts to cloud the atmosphere of a relationship, and (2) your plans to clear the air in simple straightforward conversation.

Day Four
Yielding

Old Self Instructions

Be nice, be sweet, be yielding

Sweet polite tact
Is the basis of human harmony.
So all tensions must be temperate,
Frustrations are best forgotten,
Irritations are better ignored,
Differences can be deferred,
smile, yielding is safer;
overlook it, forget it,
give up on it, sleep on it.

New Self Instructions

Be genuine, honest, real

I want a balance . . .
of honesty and openness,
of caring for and candor with,
of genuineness
and gentleness
of loving and leveling,
to excite health,
and to invite growth.

"When threatened, yield. Give in to keep the peace no matter the price."
(conflict is disastrous, try niceness)

"When challenged, sacrifice your values. Forget your concerns, put peaceful relationships above all else!"
(conflict is destructive, try placating)

"When confronted, conceal your disagreements. To differ is to reject, to disagree is a personal attack."
(conflict is divisive, smile and submit)

The two most widely used responses to impending conflict are (1) smile, quietly withdraw, blend into the background, and (2) yield to keep peace, give in to maintain relationships no matter the cost. The two styles share one conviction in common—"Mature people do not get embroiled in conflict, they keep their distance, their safe cover, their quick exit, or they give up their own goals, give in to the other's ends."

The nice guys and nice gals tend to give in almost as a reflex. For some the response was learned in a fight-shy family; for others it is the survival strategy which helped them pull through living with a volatile and abusive parent. Their perspective may be expressed in a simple "nothing is worth fighting about; the sooner you smile and go along, the better off everyone is." Or it may be a full theology of "always put others first, love sacrificially, turn the first cheek immediately and you will rarely need to turn the other."

Nice people tend to let their own needs slide, their opinions go unexpressed, their feelings remain unresolved. They may know what they want, but rarely admit it lest it damage the relationship when another disapproves of their position. In fact, they seldom take firm positions, their statements are indirect, their hope is for a relationship without difficulties. Their capacity to absorb hostility, accept injustices, adjust to others' impositions is seemingly endless.

Habitual niceness is not only painful to the self; it is also destructive to relationships. Although niceness can soothe tensions, it also generates a sense of uncertainty in others who can never be sure they will be supported in a time of crisis that demands firm support or confrontation of others. While niceness can ease a strained atmosphere, it also stifles others from giving the nice person the normal honest feedback necessary for growth. Since nice people rarely share their frustrations, those around them tend to turn their own irritations inward, generating guilt and depressive feelings among close associates. Thus chronic niceness works against that which it really seeks to preserve.

Healthful relationships nourish an equal balance of firmness and flexibility, equal support and confrontation, equal caring for another and candor with the other. Both sides are indispensable in the healthful resolution of differences and the rebuilding of relationships.

Maturity is knowing both how and when to yield, and where and why to stand firm. Maturity is discovery that one need not choose between these, that both yielding and pushing can occur together. As loving and leveling become one, then one can yield enough to keep relationships open while pressing for part or whole of one's own values and goals.

Never yielding and always yielding are both evils in human relationships. Achieving a balance of asserting one's wants and affirming one's concern for the relationship builds both affectionate and effective trust.

Dirty Fighting Code

"I'm no threat to anyone. I'd rather give in immediately than to risk rejection. I've learned to smile, absorb the abuse, look the other way, turn the other cheek, to just accept it. Sure it takes time to get over it, but somebody's got to do it; besides that's what I'm good for."

Fair Fighting Creed

"I'm a person of importance and worth. You are equally so. I will speak up for my needs, I will listen for yours. I will come to meet you halfway. I will invite you to move toward me. Let's meet in the middle."

Exercises

1. Recall the three most recent times when you avoided conflict by yielding the field and withdrawing.
   a. What kind of situations would you rather avoid?
   b. How do you feel about yourself when you have left?
   c. What is the effect on the relationship when you disappear?
2. Recall the three most recent situations when you yielded reflexively, hopelessly, or "sweetly."
   a. What feelings remained inside you afterward?
   b. What impact did it have on the ongoing relationship?
   c. What do you do with the resentment or hurt left behind?

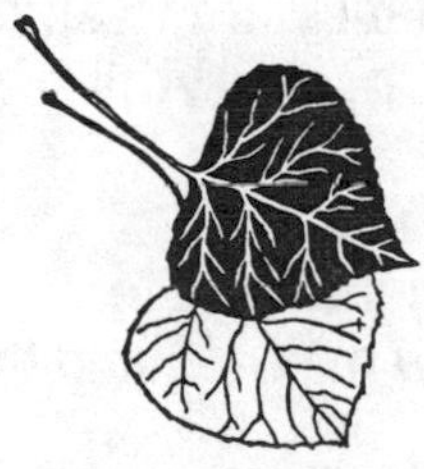

Day Five
Fogging

Old Self Instructions

Filibuster, fog, fume

Monopolize the time,
Inflate both facts and feelings.
Amplify pitch, volume, tone.
Agree with anything to evade.
Deluge them with data.
Overstate your case.
Overload the emotions.
Overwhelm their defenses.

New Self Instructions

Seek equal communications

I will respect your right
to be equally heard.
I want to hear you.

I will claim my right
to be equally heard.
I want you to hear me.

"I'm afraid of what the other may say, my position is weak, so I'm talking faster, leaving no pauses, permitting no interruption or response."
(I'm filling all airspace, snowing the other with words)

"If I just smile, nod, absorb the criticism I hear in your words, if I admit that it is possible, accept it as probable, I can go on doing what I want to anyway."
(I'm fogging by agreeing with everything without intending to do anything)

"The more you talk, the farther away I feel, I'd like to just sit silently with you for a few minutes and then let's try again."
(words can be a wall, an impenetrable barrier to communication)

Words can be used to connect, to contact, to communicate. But their function in times of conflict is frequently the reverse. Then words may serve to distance, to separate, to escape others.

As conflict threatens or breaks open, anxiety exaggerates the coping behaviors which normally serve us well, and our strengths can become weaknesses, our best skills can turn to liabilities.

The inquisitive person who can probe insightfully may become a relentless questioner when defensiveness rises. An articulate expressive person can become exaggeratedly verbose. The uses of words to shield or to screen, to mystify or to confuse, to mislead or to seduce are deeply ingrained defenses in the human personality. Filibustering, monologuing, launching into long discussions or digressions, storytelling, constantly claiming the floor, restating one's case in repetitious cycles, all serve to dominate the conversation and control the relationship.

As tension increases, both the ability to listen accurately and the capacity to communicate clearly decrease. Both the listener and the communicator must be able to move beyond the self to see as the other sees, to express what the other can perceive. Under stress, persons tend to transmit but not to receive, to broadcast but not tune in to the other's signal.

Filibustering—the art of using all available time for secondary or irrelevant talk so the real concerns cannot be dealt with—is not the sole right of legislators; it is practiced daily by a major percentage of the populace.

Fogging—the art of giving soft, shapeless, agreeable responses that actually say nothing at all—is an equally alienating way of screening oneself with words. In fogging, one agrees with the other's criticism ("Yes, it was irresponsible of me to stay out so late last night. Have I told you how much I enjoyed the party?") while continuing to think, feel, act as before. Or one agrees with the truth of another's argument ("I'm sure you're right, however I see my case as unique") while going on one's own way. An effective fogger is as elusive as a fogbank, and as unavailable to genuine encounter or real resolution of any difference.[3]

Fussing—that repetitious, negative, spiral of words that worry an old issue like a dog shaking an old rag or rat—can kick up a dust cloud of irritability between persons by the simple power of repeating, reviewing, and restating self. With couples the dialogue frequently runs:

He: I can't believe that you (yak, yak, yak).

She: Well that was because you (blah, blah, blah).

He: But didn't you hear my (yak, yak, yak)?

She: Would you do something about (blah, blah, blah)?

He: Well it has to begin with (yak, yak, yak).

She: How could that happen before (blah, blah, blah)?

So the negative cycle of stating and restating oneself, without dealing with the other's agenda, interlocks in a permanent, slowly tightening spiral of fussing, fuming, and failing to touch each other.

Effective resolution begins with a foundational commitment to seek equal communication. When each is pledged to equal hearing, equal time, equal self-disclosing of wants and needs, then filibustering stops as soon as the speaker recognizes that a lecture has begun. Fogging decreases as both press for real contact, and cyclical fussing is seen as the tired dance that it actually is, and communication begins again.

Dirty Fighting Code

"I can out-dance, outthink, outwit, outtalk, out-argue another just as soon as I get a word in edgewise."

Fair Fighting Creed

"I pledge equal communications. I will hear your concerns, I will press until mine are heard; I will listen for your feelings, I will risk sharing mine."

Exercises

1. Deliberately filibuster by talking continuously for several minutes in a conflict situation with an intimate friend, then stop and reflect aloud with the other person. "What was I doing to you by going on and on? What did it do to block or aid in the resolution of the difference we were discussing? Was it a new or an old behavior for

me? Are there other ways I avoid equal communication?"

2. Watch for any signs of fogging in your more tense interactions. Do you agree to get another off your case? Go along in word knowing that you will not agree in fact? Do you like the effect this has on the relationship?
3. Can you chart any of the cycles you get caught in with intimates? Watch for the 'tis-'taint, or yak yak/blah blah cycles in which each restates the self again and again. Can you break it by first listening to and repeating the other's point of view until s/he feels truly heard?

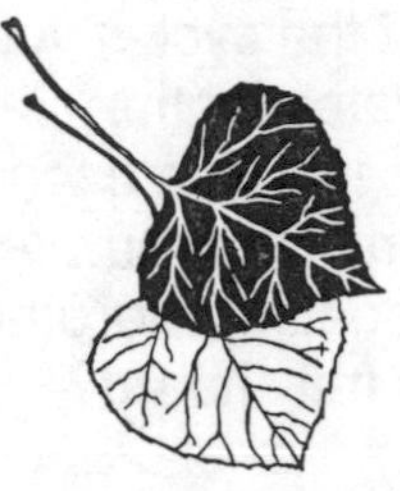

Day Six
Mystifying

Old Self Instructions

Ramble, chain react, mystify

Learn to move quickly
from issue to issue.
Ramble to confuse,
Meander to evade.
Switch quickly to mystify.
Chain react to
overwhelm.
Keep multiple complaints
going.
If one falters, flee to
another.

New Self Instructions

Seek mutual participation

One issue at a time
(I will wait
until you feel heard).
One beef at a time
(I will work
until we both
understand).
One argument at a time
(I will seek
for us both to win).

"Yes, I object to that, and another thing that reminds me of is . . ."
(ramble; never stay with one issue too long, the other may come up with a winning argument)

"I object to your behavior yesterday and I don't like what you're doing now, and another thing that gets to me is . . ."
(chain react; one issue leads to another, one irritation provokes another)

"There's no point in telling you what I'm really angry about, but it would help if you'd at least do something about . . ."
(mystify; keep multiple complaints afloat, switch rapidly between issues so the other is always confused)

Blessed with a good memory and a fine attention to detail, the rambler can move interestingly from theme to theme, issue to issue, irritation to irritation, dropping a hint here, a threat there and moving on before a response is possible. Then if the other wishes to reply it can be denied or evaded by saying that wasn't the real issue.

Endowed with the capacity to link together incidents, issues, and items that are distractingly vague and at the same time anxiety-arousing, the chain reactor can flit from circumstance to intentional slight to happenstance to intentional injury to incidental occurrence to incendiary irritation. The other party to the conversation feels attacked from all sides, then turns to discover there is no one there. The chain reactor's fancy footwork allows him/her to dance away and proceed to critique from the rear.

But the supreme talent is to truly mystify. This

includes the ability to critique in creative generalization or suggest an issue covertly while not overtly revealing it; the art of triggering a conflict without actually initiating it; the knack of acting out frustration while blithely denying it exists; the strategy of setting the other up for a positive stroke then offering something neutral or negative; the game of building up the other's hopes then pulling the rug out from under him/her. The list of mystifications is endless. The effect of such moves and countermoves is eventually crazy-making.

The old self instructions that guide such clever dance steps are a blend of fear and anger. The fear of a direct frank confrontation. "I will not be heard. I will be devalued as a person, overwhelmed in the conflict, reduced to silence, tears, shame. I am angry that I cannot be heard, valued, recognized as equal. I am even angrier at the outcomes I fear would follow if I risked open debate. I must hit and run, ambush and escape."

The past models that shape the mystifying-rambling-meandering dance were internalized early. They are learned so effectively because they frustrate so deeply. Complex patterns of mystifying behavior which are as intricate as a dramatic plot are incorporated into automatic response-sequences and acted out without a hitch. The very conflict styles which are hated in the family of origin are so thoroughly ingrained that they rise with the first instincts of self-protection. Such behaviors threaten so deeply that they frequently are attached to the unconscious survival impulses, so they are invested with life and death energy. Change then comes more slowly and begins with very small steps. Awareness is the key. Then one can stop when feeling the panic that lies behind an impulse to mystify the other with multi-level communications, multiple-choice statements, and ask, "What am I feeling, what do I want, how can I express it simply and clearly?"

The goal of change is to seek mutual, equal involvement in any conflict negotiated. For this to be possible, one must deal with one issue at a time and be patient until the other hears or feels heard. One must present one beef—objection—at a time, and work with it until both understand its impact and importance. One must pursue only one argument at a time and seek for a mutually satisfactory solution in which neither loses, both win.

Dirty Fighting Code

"I am powerless, unless I take him/her by surprise; I am helpless unless I can stay off the spot, out of the corner, one step ahead; this conflict is hopeless unless I outthink, outstep, outwit the other."

Fair Fighting Creed

"I will listen to my own wants, fears, feelings and share them as I become aware of them. I will listen for your needs, hopes, emotions and honor them as I hear them, one thought, one feeling, one step, one change at a time."

Exercises

Try these three experiences for a day and keep notes on your discoveries.

1. When I ramble off I will stop—as soon as I recognize it and report, "I'm rambling."
2. When I note that I am chain-reacting I will stop myself, reflect quietly for a moment to find what one thing I really want.
3. When I mystify I will feel my own confusion and report it.

Day Seven
Generalizing

Old Self Instructions

Generalize, universalize, exaggerate

Do not speak of a single instance—
Generalize on patterns of behavior
"you always," "you never," "you're forever."
Do not speak of one person—
Universalize on human behavior
"you're like all men," "that's a woman for you."
Do not speak of the actual extent—
Exaggerate to increase the impact
"you don't care at all," "you demand perfection."

New Self Instructions

Focus, center, simplify

Define the conflict narrowly—
Focus on the actual act, the present instance at stake.
Define the conflict neutrally—
Clarify, simplify, specify.
Reduce to the smallest unit of behavior.
Define the conflict naturally—
Center on the persons present
And the particular behaviors in question.

"Why must you always say never?"

"I wish you would never say always!"

(ultimate language—using always, never, forever—"invariably" triggers resentment or resistance)

"That's a man for you!"

"That was said just like a woman!"

(generalizing from one person to all persons in a group, gender, or class misuses the one and misjudges the whole)

"I can't explain it. I mean to say six, but it comes out sixty-six."

(exaggerating, whether for argumentative impact or for emotional effect, inflates the data, fires feelings, and defeats its own goals)

Exaggerating, generalizing, universalizing are power plays. When anxiety rises we tend to swing from mature uses of power—the "power to" act, choose, negotiate, to immature forms of power—the "power over" another. Resorting to such strategies is not only a vote of nonconfidence for your own observation or position, it is also a sign of doubt of one's own power. The marginal notes of a minister's sermon reveal this. "Point weak, raise voice, pound pulpit, if audience is not moved, wipe eyes with handkerchief."

When we regress to the desperation of attempting "power over," then the manipulation of facts and the enlarging of their importance promises the intimidation of the other, and we rarely gain the desired power, since such strategies create their own defeat. Relationships which depend on power over, or being overpowered, are unhealthful to either the dominating or the submitting partner, to the validator or the invalid. In healthful relationships, neither person is reduced to meet the other's needs. Both are invited to grow in the interactions of communication and the transactions of the friendship contract. Such friendships respect each party's power to be, to think, to feel, to choose, to respond as a responsible self.

The direction of "power over" is to enlarge, inflate, involve greater, more complex arguments. The definition of issues in conflict are made as large, as foreboding, as all-inclusive as possible. To define a conflict with a marriage partner as a difference in how we keep schedules is resolvable. But to see the other as being untrustworthy, unable to keep all covenants, irresponsible with all relationships, insensitive to anyone else's feelings, and having just ruined the marriage is unsolvable. To see an act of disobedience by a student as a single issue to be negotiated is manageable. But to see it as the rebellion of youth, the generation gap, the triumph of the new morality, the decline and fall of Western civilization and a sign of the end of the age is beyond management.

"Power to" moves in the opposite direction, seeking to focus the conflict, find the center of the issue, specify the problem, simplify its dynamics until both can get a handle on what is happening. Power to act increases as the conflict is defined more sharply, simply, clearly. How it is defined is the key factor on the direction the conflict will take. Defining it in an increasing spiral of enlarging arguments moves toward prolonged or abortive conflict. Resolution lies in the opposite direction.

The three key secrets in definition are:

One. Define the conflict narrowly. Focus on the single act. Break down the situation to the actual behavior that is in question. Stay with the act, fact, instance you want to see changed. Refuse to generalize. Avoid ultimate language. State no universals.

Two. Define the conflict neutrally. Clarify in nonoffensive language, simplify with mutually acceptable terms, specify with verbs. Refuse labeling nouns; use adverbs which deal with quantity, discard adjectives which picture qualities; describe, don't evaluate; say how much in more-or-less-language, not what kind in concrete good/bad, nice/rude judgments. Refuse to exaggerate, inflate, escalate.

Three. Define the conflict naturally. Center on the persons present and the ways conflict rises naturally in the relationship between them. Some conflicts rise from within a single person but they occur between at least two. To see it as a mutual difficulty to be resolved jointly so both win is most productive.

Dirty Fighting Code

Feel powerless? Enlarge the issue, inflate the facts. Engage the other in a bigger and bigger battle. Show them how significant, how infuriating, how intolerable the situation is. There are no little hassles!

Fair Fighting Creed

Keep it simple, keep it small, keep it focused, keep it clear, keep it specific.

Exercises

Reflect on a recent conflict issue. Focus on the bone of contention.

1. Now enlarge, exaggerate, generalize, make universal judgments about the other and all such situations. Be aware of the feelings, judgments, and impulses to act which emerge.
2. Now pause, center, sit silently for a moment.

Then focus, reduce, clarify, define the conflict as narrowly, neutrally, naturally as possible. Compare feelings, contrast the direction your impulses lead. What have you learned from this experience?

Day Eight
Analyzing

Old Self Instructions	**New Self Instructions**
Analyze, intellectualize, advise	***Own my part in our pain***
Analyze the other's shortcomings. Critique the other's behavior. Evaluate the other's choices. (if she disagrees, it proves you were right) Advise, to show it's their problem. Help, to keep it at their doorstep. Rescue with a vengeance. (you're only doing it for his/her own good)	I will own my part In our two-person problem. When I analyze I'm fleeing my fear. When I intellectualize I'm fleeing my pain. When I advise I'm fingering the other.

"Have you noticed that the very things you object to in me, you are fighting in yourself?"
(touché; when I analyze you I keep attention off myself; when I point out your problems I am evading mine)

"I'm not your father, although you were obviously using me to work out the old authority problems that belong between you and him."
(bravo! when I intellectualize, I have escaped real encounter; I have danced out of reach, I am emotionally out of touch)

"I suggest you tease out the demands inside your anger and either assert them or cancel them."
(right on! when I advise I'm fingering your problem and forgetting mine)

The most common response to another's confrontation is evaluation. The immediate flight to judgments allows the judge to rise above, or pretend to be above, the vulnerable position criticism creates.

The most habitual response to a problematic relationship is to analyze the other's part and advise the other to change. The real benefits of analysis are not for the one being analyzed but for the analyst. When analyzing, a whole series of illusions are created. The analysis process subtly suggests that (1) the problem in the relationship lies in the other person; (2) I can see it with clarity while s/he is blind to its nature; (3) I can tell the other how to change if s/he will only listen; (4) the problem will vanish if the other will shape up as I prescribe. The reverse is equally and at times exclusively true. The analyst is frequently observing the effects not the cause (which lies in the self), critiquing the reflection not the reality (which is the hidden anger being projected on the other).

Three classic phenomena occur in this process.

One. The mirror-image reflection: In conflict it is incredibly common for both parties to believe "I am an innocent victim representing truth and justice while being evilly attacked."

Two. The mote-beam mechanism: One party can see all the "vicious underhanded acts" of the other party, but is blind to identical acts engaged in by the self. "I'm sick and tired of your nagging. You are always cutting me down, you crank." Note the beam in the critic's eye while pointing out the mote in the other's eye, as Jesus unforgettably described it.

Three. The double standard distortion: Even if both of us are aware of our identical acts, there is a strong tendency to judge that "what is all right for me to do to you, if I can, is not all right for you to do to me! In fact what I am doing to you is good, obviously. And what you are doing to me is bad, undeniably!"[4]

All three of these phenomena spring from the impulse to critique, analyze, and evaluate. To reduce them, one must unhook from the self-defensive cycles until each is seen as worthful, valued, distinct in his or her own right. As each takes full responsibility for his or her own boundaries and refuses to analyze, criticize, or rescue the other, a new respect is born.

Out of years of analyzing to gain "advantage," these learnings emerge. When I analyze another, no matter how accurate the hunch, I am escaping something fearful in myself. When I scrutinize another, no matter how clear the perceptions, I am fleeing something puzzling in myself. When I evaluate another, no matter how right the judgments, I am escaping something painful in myself. When I advise another, no matter how wise the directions, I am avoiding something uncomfortable in myself.

Wisdom begins to occur in human beings as they focus on their own part in any two-person problems, analyze their own contribution to any multiple-person hassles, reflect on their own pain and fear and its impact on the relationship.

A marriage grows as each person gets off the other's case and lets him/her be, gets out of the other's hair and lets him/her grow, quits shaking the other's family tree and works only on his or her own.

A friendship grows as each takes care of his or her half of the interaction and risks sharing what is valued, wanted, hoped for; it falters when either begins to analyze or advise.

Dirty Fighting Code

"I will judge first before I can be judged by the other, analyze immediately before I can be labeled by the other's analysis. He who defines, wins. She who validates is never an invalid."

Fair Fighting Creed

"I will own my part in our two-person problem, examine my contribution to any painful interaction, change my position toward any binding relationship."

Exercises

Finish the following statements in as many ways as occur to you.

1. When I evaluate another, I am feeling . . .
2. When I analyze my friend or partner, I am fearing . . .
3. When I criticize another, I am hurting from . . .
4. When I advise others, the payoff is . . .

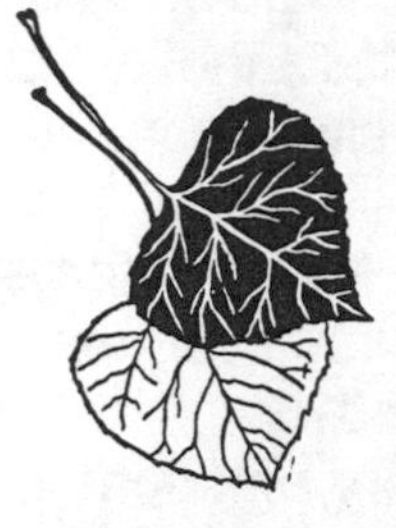

Day Nine
Binding

Old Self Instructions

Activate ambivalences

Watch for conflicting feelings
And point them out to the other.
Note any contradictions
And highlight them for another.
Use his words to disprove his point.
Set her thoughts against herself.
Mix up emotions to split feelings.
Polarize views to confuse perceptions.

New Self Instructions

One side at a time

The thoughts I think are mine,
No matter how conflicted.
The feelings I feel are mine,
No matter how mixed.
The views I hold are mine,
No matter how contrary.
For these I am fully responsible.
Your thoughts and feelings,
Your values and views,
Are yours no matter the contradictions.
For them you are fully responsible.

"Look, I want to go and I don't. I'd really like to see my family, and that's the last place I want to be!"
(two opposite feelings can reside in the same heart)

"It's all right, let's just forget it ever happened and go on. But don't you ever ask me to borrow my camper again, understand?"
(two contradictory emotions can shape one's actions as well as fire one's emotions)

"He's the only man I'll ever love, I want him back; but if he walks through that door I'm afraid I'll kill him."
(two powerful urges can coexist, two wills wrestle within the heart)

No one ever totally loves another person. Love and hate coexist within the heart, but in varying degrees. For most of us love may fill even 95 percent of experienced emotion, but the 5 percent of unlove—hate if you dare call it what it is—lurks to swell in times of disappointment or disgust until it reaches competitive proportions.

No one can totally admire another. Admiration is always mixed with resentment. We both admire and resent those who excel in areas we aspire to reach. We may largely admire, and yet the resentment is still there to rise when another succeeds, or to rejoice a bit when the other is inconvenienced.

So love/hate, admiration/resentment, attraction/repulsion, stability/mobility, all are there within us. And in those around us. Emotions are mingled streams. It is the nature of human feeling.

And so we are vulnerable to those who seek to hook our hidden feelings, play our ambivalences, rouse our buried other side, because another side is always there. Only when it is claimed—not denied, appreciated—not feared, can we smile as either or both sides emerge, knowing that they are parts of our inner whole.

Dirty fighters have an instinct for such things and hardly need the long introduction just given. The intuitive sense of where a person's feelings are split, loyalties are divided, thoughts are contradictory, allows the fighter to play them one against the other.

Of all the behaviors that cut at another's core nothing is more diabolic than to divide and conquer, to set his feelings against themselves, to use her words to disprove her point, to pit his thoughts in opposition, to mix up emotions and thus pull the rug from under his or her feet.

To divide another's feelings by exposing the other pole which lies hidden to them is a manipulation most foul when used to gain one's own ends. Divide and conquer becomes a dictum for a personal attack. Training in listening skills and counseling methods can make this a special temptation. In the helping relationship one calls out the ambivalent feelings to invite the other to claim the whole of oneself, to experience both positive and negative poles. But using such skills to defeat or dismay another is destructive to both the meddler and the meddled.

Effective conflict resolution begins with each dealing with but one side at a time, one's own side. The first requisite is the discipline to own one's thoughts—no matter how conflicted; to prize one's feelings—no matter how mixed; to affirm one's values and views—no matter how contrary, and to claim full responsibility for all of them.

And when it comes to the other's mixed, confused, conflicted emotions and convictions, the appropriate response is invitation, not manipulation. To invite another to further self-disclose, to claim more of the self, to risk being more real can move the conflict toward greater contact. But to maneuver the sides of a person against him/herself offers little but confusion.

Dirty Fighting Code

Divide and conquer. Set side against side, pole against pole, fear against fear. The winner gains an inner advantage.

Fair Fighting Creed

"I will deal with my ambivalence and not use yours; I will appreciate my mixed motives and not depreciate yours; I will recognize my confusion and not seek to create, excite, exploit yours!"

Exercises

Reflect on three key relationships and claim both poles of your emotions to appreciate more fully the richness of your feelings, the complexity of your humanness. Finish these lines for each:

1. I appreciate and I resent ____________________.
2. I prize and I despise ____________________.
3. I want more __________ and I don't want any more ____________________.

   What new parts of your inner richness do you discover?

   What fears emerge, what pain do you uncover?

Day Ten

Gunnysacking

Old Self Statements

Gunnysack grievances

Collect hurts,
Accumulate slights.
Remember injustices.
Brood on injuries.
When loaded to the gills
Get it off your chest.
(Keep grievances on file
to balance any losses
or justify any acts.)

New Self Statements

Deal with here and now

I will finish my anger
at past predicaments of
failure.
I will cancel my anger
of future predictions of
failure.
I will work through
the anger felt here,
I will open the future
to risk being real now.

"Once, I could overlook, twice, hurt. The third time I could hardly hold it in, but this is too much!"
(I'm keeping score and you've struck out)

"Now that you asked, yes, you have done it before. Last January third to be exact, and May twelfth, and June four and six."
(I'm keeping books and you're in the red)

"I never bring up the past, I wouldn't think of dragging out old laundry, but I remember, how could one forget?"
(I'm keeping it in and it's slowly eating away)

Of all the collectables, injuries are the most widely saved and carefully treasured items, and they are the most expensive. The cost of carrying a set of open accounts for those about you is (1) ongoing brooding, (2) unfinished business, (3) overloaded emotions, (4) past distances separating any present encounter, (5) fear and suspicion toward the future, (6) bodily complaints as the stress is converted to physical symptoms, (7) exaggeration of new difficulties caused by adding in old accounts, (8) caution about new persons who remind you of remembered injustices, and (9) the energy required for all of the above. These rob one of what might have been.

Gunnysacking grievances is carrying complaints along quietly for any length of time until the bag bursts. Then the dated irritations, retouched by the other negative memories with which they were stored, spill out in a rush of anger. The trigger for such explosions is frequently a trivial incident which would have been a minor disappointment had not the reservoir of anger already been brimming.

Gentle gunnysacking can occur inadvertently as trivia accumulate which are dismissed as "not worth fighting about," and get suppressed in the interest of domestic peace or good working relationships. Eventually they boil over when the limit is reached.

General gunnysacking as a way of deliberately dealing with anger is a more studied process, usually learned in one's family of origin and following predictable patterns for each person. The more common is (1) accumulation—quietly adding new grievances without any outward sign, (2) clue dropping—as the collection is nearing capacity, (3) explosion—when some incident provides the occasion, excuse, or exasperation, (4) ventilation—when the history is reviewed, (5) withdrawal—without effective closure, the gunnysacker feels a sense of release, but reclaims the agenda for future use, (6) contrition—the lid of self-blame goes back on and the person passively seeks to appease the other for the outburst or actively warns and blames the other for its occurrence.

Clue dropping is a flashing danger signal indicating that the gunnysack is ballooning and about to tear. Typical clues are: "You know we never talk," "You've got to stop doing that," or "Don't push me too far," or "I wish you'd stop ignoring me." At this point a frank, level, "Come on now, what's going on with you?" may open the collection deliberately rather than waiting for some tension to spark a fire.

The most effective intervention must start much earlier in the process, at the beginning where the picking up of gripes begins. Effective fighting happens between persons who stay up-to-date with their bookkeeping. The books on important relationships can be balanced daily, much as a bank keeps credits and debits current by clearing all checks before closing down every evening. The wisdom "to not let the sun go down upon your wrath" as the Apostle Paul counseled, can be practiced personally in cancelling old accounts in a deliberate act of finishing the old business or in joint conversations that lay the offending situation to rest.

At the heart of up-to-date ledgers lies the commitment to finish anger as immediately and appropriately as possible. Sustaining anger over long periods is painful, exhausting, and destructive to the body since the human psyche tends to lodge it in organs other than the brain.

Accepting one's humanity realistically sets one free from some of anger's most painful pretentions. We cannot undo the past. What is formed cannot be reformed, it can only be transformed now in creative resolution of its continuing results. The past is past. So it will always be. Finishing demands on past predicaments is a first sign of real wisdom. The future is equally inaccessible. One cannot control the uncontrollable. Cancelling demands which seek to control tomorrow with ironclad guarantees or shape it with future predictions sets one more free to live now.

If there is to be any real change, it must happen now. If there is to be any true reconciliation, it must take place here.

Dirty Fighting Code

"I saw that, I felt that, I'll save that. I'll use it when I'm good and ready. Meanwhile, I'll let it grow inside me until the right time for it comes along!"

Fair Fighting Creed

"I will let go of what was, let be what is, let come what will. Each day's anger is sufficient for that day. I will carry over as little as possible from day to day."

Exercises

1. Review the costs of gunnysacking in paragraph 1 of this section. How many of the nine effects have you experienced in observing others? In feelings of bitterness you carried?
2. Reflect on the cycle of collecting. Where do you interrupt the process in yourself? When you begin dropping clues? When the first items get internalized? How can you intervene?
3. Finish these lines "I resent . . . "; "I am continually bothered by . . . "; "A bone I'd like to pick is . . . " What do you discover?

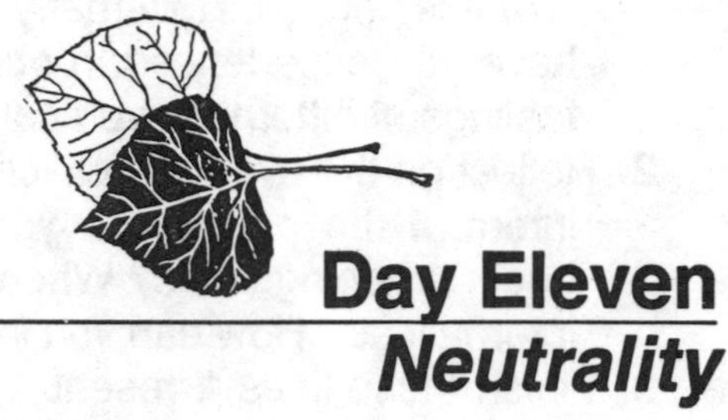

Day Eleven
Neutrality

Old Self Instructions	**New Self Instructions**
Be silent, superior, neutral	***Be open, present, available***
"Silence" is strength (be unavailable). Stonewall by keeping mum (don't get hooked).	"Silence" is violence, Openness is strength. Risk! Share!
"Superiority" is security (be unreachable). Stay cool, stay uncommitted (don't get involved).	"Superiority" is flight. Presence is Power. Hurt? Heal!
"Neutrality" is safety (be untouchable). Rise above the situation (don't touch or be touched).	Neutrality is numbness. Contact is aliveness. Touch! Feel!

"I refuse to get involved in petty conflicts, they're beneath my pride."
(from up here where I sit, it's not important)

"I've learned that silence is not only golden, it's the better part of wisdom.
(no comment)

"We who seek to live rationally must maintain an appropriate neutrality in the face of adversity."
(this is your personal computer speaking . . .)

"And the computer created man in its own image and likeness, male and female created it them and said, 'Be perfectly rational, be objectively neutral.' And the computer said, 'Affirmative.' "

The temptation is great to escape from the tensions, anxieties, and uncertainties of life by becoming a computer. When life is only a program, the options seem more predictable, more manageable. The creator and the created computer become more and more alike.

The attraction of neutrality is great for those who trust in objectivity and rationality as the ultimate solution to human difficulties. There are moments when maintaining a neutral position are highly useful, such as when mediating between two hostile parties, or when listening to another ventilate uncontrolled emotions. A cool head behind an understanding face can draw off hostility and invite others to see and hear each other with greater clarity.

But when engaged in a disagreement with another, neutrality evokes mistrust. Any appearance of being superior, neutral, indifferent, reduces trust sharply. Trust is evoked by people who describe what they see, not evaluate or judge; by those who are spontaneous and natural, not using strategies and manipulative methods; by those who show empathy and involvement, not neutrality and disinterest; by those who exhibit equality and closeness, not superiority and distance.

Using strategies of concealed means or ambiguous motives to gain the desired outcome elicits mistrust. Showing neutrality when feelings get tense appears as a lack of interest and real involvement which stimulates mistrust. Communicating a sense of superior power, ability or resources creates distance and inspires immediate suspicion.

When moving out of reach into neutrality, most persons use distance—physically, emotionally, relationally—at the very time when trust, contact, support are most needed. They become unavailable, unreachable, untouchable.

Silence is not necessarily strength. The stereotype of the strong-silent type is most frequently found to be a tower of weakness. The "strength" that depends on silent avoidance of involvement becomes highly vulnerable when someone scales the walls and penetrates the defenses.

Superiority is no guarantee of security. Any attempt to move vertically evokes any authority problems unfinished in the other and adds them to the present issue. Seeking to play parent, act as an authority or attempt policing causes at least equal tension as it provides leverage.

Neutrality is a temporary safety. The stability of genuine relationship comes from trustworthy covenanting, mutual contracting; and these require involvement if they are to have any depth.

If in threat you tend to become a computer, withdrawing into the precise, overly objective manner of the totally rational woman or man, then plan to use your own strength to move toward a new balance. Become aware of the bodily posture you assume in times of threat. Do you sit back, straighten and stiffen the spine, tense the jaw, lift the chin? Be aware of the emotional stance you assume. Do you become very reasonable, rational, clinical in language and argument? Be aware of the beliefs which lie behind the behaviors. Typically these are:

"All debate must be perfectly reasonable since logic is the last word. Feelings must have a rational justification before they dare be expressed. Spontaneity is limited, impulsive responses are compulsively edited, intuitions are discounted, feelings belittled, people become correct computers."

From awareness can come the deliberate choice to return to discover the feelings; to feel the fears, hurts and angers, to know the impatience, irritation and frustration, to savor the tenderness, affection and gentleness.

Then share them. Risk new openness, allow the joy and pain to mingle, let the hurt and healing mingle, touch others and be touched; let yourself feel more deeply. Wholeness is the real goal, insight and intuition, thought and feeling, fact and hunch are equally important. Both contribute to our humanness, both complete human community.

Dirty Fighting Code

"I've nothing to say, you can struggle with it alone. I'm not available for your hassle, it's your problem. I've no feelings at all about what is going wrong between us, if there is any change to be made, it's up to you."

Fair Fighting Creed

"I will be open to hear your pain, I will equally honor mine. I will be present, available, involved in my part of our two-person problems. I will respect your right to and responsibility for your part.

Exercises

1. Reread the three levels of awareness. If you tend to compute, note which one is your growing edge at this moment.
2. If you negotiate with, work with, are married to a "neutral, superior, or silent" person who becomes a computer in conflict, reread the awareness assignments. How can you invite "the other side" out of the other person in times of tension? Plan a step, think of the words you would use, rehearse the sentence.

Day Twelve
Angering

Old Self Instructions

Hide anger—ventilate rage

Don't admit to anger
When denial is possible
(I'm not angry, I'm just concerned.)
Don't give them the satisfaction
Of knowing that they got to you.
(I'm not angry, I'm above that!)
Then blow up when they least expect it
Or don't get mad, get even.

New Self Instructions

Own anger clearly

I will own my anxiety,
Accept my anger,
Admit my irritation,
Describe my demands,
Assert those that are just,
Cancel those that are unfair
So that my arousal
Will both clear the air
And show I care.

"I'm not angry, you're the one that's upset. I'd suggest you cool down and listen to reason."
(ignore the anger in yourself, point out the anger in another)

"I wouldn't give her the satisfaction of making me upset. I can smile and take it for now."
(hide your own anger, infuriate the other by being doubly nice, utterly kind; shame her with your unselfishness)

"One more nasty word, and I'll give him what he's asking for, I wouldn't do it if he didn't have it coming."
(it's all his fault, by his invitation, it's not my responsibility)

There is a wealth of puzzling attitudes toward this puzzling emotion.

"Anger is evil, deny it." This moralistic view sees anger as a sign of the dangerous bestiality that lurks in the hearts of humans and must be contained, controlled, concealed at any cost. Some anger is malignant and evil, but not all.

"Anger is an attack, suppress it." This fearful view rises from all those experiences of vicious attacking anger and rightfully recognizes that the impulse to injure must be suppressed. But it mistakenly assumes that the one kind of anger—destructive rage—is the only kind.

"Anger is immaturity, outgrow it." This superior view is partly true. Much anger rises from childish fantasy, from early illusions of omnipotence, from global demands with godlike pretentions.

"Anger is power, assert it." This self-centered view has one pole of truth, but ignores the other. There are situations in which energy in anger can supply the needed motivation to demand the appropriate change. But anger is power when it supports justice, it is not power in itself. Anger for angry-power's sake boomerangs.

"Anger is self-destructive, ventilate it." This therapeutic view is true only of some angers. Those who internalize rage in the body and live with bottled up rage can develop various symptoms—ulcers, arthritis, colitis, hypertension—to name some of the most common. The cyclical process needs interruption, but this is no basis for encouraging us all to ventilate all angry impulses. Ventilation increases anger for most personalities, it does not decrease or dissipate the energy as is commonly cited. Angry ventilation, like a negative spiral, stimulates further anger emotions.

"Anger is arousal, manage it, direct it." This behavioral view has the support of all research done on natural groups of people. The other views are based on studies of those who come for help on physical symptoms, emotional stress, or cyclical rage. Anger is the bodily arousal which occurs when one appraises a relationship or situation with frustrated demands. To appreciate the arousal as a sign of aliveness, to accept it as a normal sign of emotional investment, to admit that it is present without hiding it from yourself, to choose either to express the frustrated demands or to cancel them is inappropriate.

Anger, then, is the emotional arousal surrounding demands. Within each of us there exists layer on layer of demands learned in childhood, shaped in youth, tested in adult years. Some of the demands are irrational, all out of proportion to the situation. These can be owned and, with proper humility and humor, cancelled. Other demands are core values, central beliefs that shape the personality. These are just demands that deserve expression and negotiation.

In an angry moment these demands rise to awareness and must then be recognized, sorted and either cancelled or expressed. Demands like, "Do what I want, when I want it simply because I want it," are obviously unjust. In contrast the demand, "I want to be heard. I will equally hear you, so let's be open together," is a just demand pressing for equality, and deserves to be expressed and a joint solution sought.

Once persons can own their arousal, accept their anger, admit what irritations they feel, and deal clearly with their demands, there is little likelihood that they will ventilate rage on others. The impact of clearly focused demands is far greater than the explosion of free-floating anger that bubbles out in times of ventilation of feelings. The satisfaction of finding a way to negotiate the central values at stake is far more rewarding than even the rush of adrenalin that goes with angry outbursts. Ventilating rage has been shown to offer little beyond the shock of recognition of one's own anger or that of the other. Getting it off your chest only puts it on your shoulders. One still must decide what to do about the demands that lie behind it all.

The secret of creative anger lies in owning, accepting, sorting out the demands, cancelling the 90 percent that are useless, and standing firmly with the 5 percent that are really important.

Be available to others—with both your gentle and your firm sides, with the affection and the anger. Both can be drives toward deeper relationship.

Dirty Fighting Code

"I say what I feel, whatever it is, whenever it rises. If others can't handle it, too bad."

Fair Fighting Creed

"I will own my anxiety (I get tense in conflict). I will accept my anger (I get upset by my demands). I will assert just demands (I want change). I will cancel unjust demands (I want fairness and reality)."

Exercises

1. Reflect on the six basic attitudes toward anger. Have you held different ones during different periods of your life? Which one is predominant now? Which view do you want to hold and assimilate into your feelings?
2. Think of anger-arousal situation from the recent past. Write out the demands that you felt. Explore the irrational, exaggerated demands that rise in impulse. Clarify the central just demands—if there are such. Reflect on how you cancel or assert these.

Day Thirteen
Rumoring

Old Self Instructions

Play detective

Keep a file for future use.
Listen in on the phone extension.
Read your children's diaries.
Go through your spouse's purse.
Quiz your children's friends.
Keep your eyes open for clues.
Save any tidbits for ammunition,
Never waste it before a fight.

New Self Instructions

Refuse hearsay

Report only on recent events.
Refuse secondhand data.
Collect no anonymous stories.
Seek no covert information.
Save no painful memories.
Stay with the here and now.
Deal with firsthand experience.

"If what I heard is right and what I suspect is true then have I got the goods on you."
(playing detective promises the power of information but it proves powerless in building trust)

"I can't say who told me, but I have it from a very reliable source . . . "
(collecting hearsay is like gathering smoke, there are signs but no reality)

"How I found out is not important; what I want to know is, is it true?"
(a message with a hidden messenger is partly false; full truth requires content, context and contact between the sender and the receiver)

Gathering information, collecting rumors, hustling up hearsay are all means of amassing power. Information is one of power's many forms, and illicit information, whether borrowed, stolen or invented, can be used to overpower another in times of conflict. It is a favorite strategy for those who feel a deep need to win and an even greater need to see the other lose.

Playing detective is a favorite role for the secret information addict. Reading children's diaries can help the prying parent to collect clues and give warning cues to the kids. Going through a partner's mail, or pockets, or drawers can offer the spying spouse bits of evidence for whatever theory. Quizzing friends, keeping watch, staying alert for any compromising stories can all add to the accumulating data. These and many more ploys make up the art of rumoring.

Rumors are the coinage of community conflicts and the raw material of more intimate interactions as well. In any ambiguous situation, as anxiety arises in the atmosphere and ambivalent feelings are aroused, rumors precipitate as explanations. The spontaneous generation of rumors occurs as persons automatically pool their resources of intuition, suspicion and information. As they pass from mouth to mouth, they undergo a fascinating transformation. Rumors become shorter, more concise, more understandable and repeatable; they increase in bias as they are passed along; they take on authority as they go. People forget the source but retain the content, they hear what they want to hear and retain the desired details.

In community, the rules of rumor are:

One. If people want information, and lack it, they produce it.

Two. If people are anxious, with no explanation, rumors are constructed.

Three. The more emotionally charged a rumor is, the more likely it will be distorted, elaborated, exaggerated in passing.

Four. Once a rumor is afloat, it is more likely to spread if it matches what people expect or desire.

Five. Even after a rumor has been tested and disproven, it will be believed if it supports existing biases and beliefs.

In interpersonal conflicts, all of the above are equally true. If a person wants an explanation and none exists, suspicions rise instantly. The more anxious the worrier, the more certain the theory will feel; the more emotionally loaded, the more it will grow and incorporate other facts known or fears felt; once the rumor is alive in the thoughts, it will spread into feelings, attitudes, actions if it matches other expectations; and such fantasies have staying power, they remain to haunt us even when disproven.

To silence rumors in community, the rules are simple: (1) check the source—the subject or the object; (2) check the carrier—is it a direct observation? (3) weigh the consequences for all involved if it proves true; (4) consider the benefits the rumor offers the originator or the carrier; (5) stay close to firsthand observations, to the actual conversations with the persons involved.

The same issues arise in relationship. To reduce rumoring within or between intimates, suspend judgment on all hunches, fears, fantasies, or fragments of information. Go to the person as soon as possible, check out the facts. If your suspicion persists, ask what benefit, what consequences, what payoffs lie hidden in the hunch. Discard all secondhand stories. Cancel all hearsay as soon as possible. Healing and reconciliation come from real encounter. Seek it above all else.

Dirty Fighting Code

Sleuth out "the truth," spy out the evidence, assemble your theory. Use it to gain advantage. Life is a whodone-it.

Fair Fighting Creed

"I will make statements of observation, limit them to what I have observed, address what I actually experience in our relationship. Life is encounter."

Exercises

1. Examine the rules of rumor in community. How many of these have you experienced in church, at work, in community?
2. Explore the rules of internal rumors. Do you find these steps to suspicion occurring automatically within?
3. Write three resolutions for reducing speculation in your own thinking and speech. Check them out with a spouse or friend.

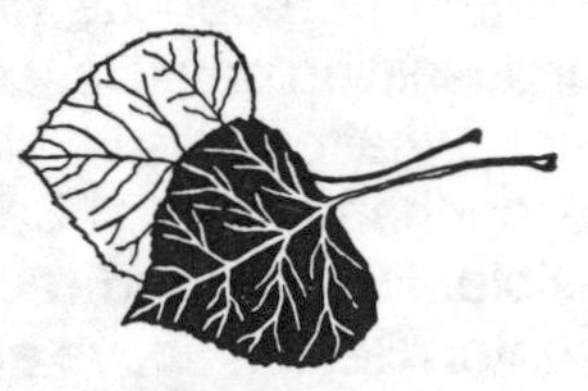

Day Fourteen
Blaming

Old Self Instructions

Blaming and shaming

Whatever goes wrong
Is somebody's fault,
Fix the blame.
Whenever something
fails
Someone must suffer.
Stir up shame
(quick before you get
blamed)
(better them than you
shamed).

New Self Instructions

Affirming responsibility

You are responsible
For whatever you do.
You are never to blame.
We are each responsible
For whatever we do.
We need not feel shame.

"Don't look at me, I didn't start this one. It's all your fault the evening was a disaster."
(in an ongoing relationship, there are no beginnings and no ends since each communication comments on what preceded, anticipates what is to follow)

"If you hadn't said (done, acted, looked) as you did, none of this hassle would have happened."
(it's your problem, it's your fault, it's your immaturity; what a relief to lay it all at your doorstep)

"I would think you'd be more than a little ashamed after the scene in the restaurant in front of your friends."
(actually you were more genuinely assertive than usual, but I'm threatened by your new strength)

The most common block to effective communication is the tendency to act as "prosecutor." From the moment one or both begin to fix blame and prove guilt, the relationship is in trouble.

Blaming is a system of avoiding responsibility. The impulse to blame, and the escape it promises, make it the most common as well as the most ancient escape from responsibility. In the Eden story, Adam's first instinct is an intricate triple blame maneuver. (It's the woman, the snake, and you, God, who created them.)

The blamer with the accusingly pointed finger has found the most convenient way to excuse himself of all responsibility, or escape detection of her part in the problem: Finger the foe. Fix the blame. Assign the guilt. Define whose problem it is. Lay the full responsibility at the other's doorstep. If the partner willingly grovels, the interaction is complete. Every blamer seeks a placater; every guilty victim, a tyrant. It takes two to continue these cyclical psychodramas. It takes one to quit.

The need to blame rises from the fear of being blamed. Those who frequently blame others are avoiding the pain of the chronic inner conflict between a blaming tyrant and a bleeding victim. Rather than suffer the attacks of the ruthless censor preying on the self, one turns the blame outward.

Before raising the condemning finger, the blamer feels blame within. To follow this urge to punish the self is intolerable so the punishment is turned outward. This rage against all inconvenience, all failure, all imperfection, all that goes wrong in life flares instantly and urgently within, flashes in the eyes and burns in the words. Why feel blamed when you can blame?

Blame is evasive. Rather than facing the difficulty and work at resolving it, it seeks transfer of the total to the other, to stir up shame, pain, self-rejection in the other hoping to stimulate self-correction by the other. Such negative means produce negative feelings and lead to negative results. Growth comes from owning responsibility, not from accepting blame.

Blame is censure. Rather than pointing toward the future and inviting change and growth, blame penalizes the past and punishes the person for the acts, whether real or fantasized. Change and healing come from responsibility thinking, not from figuring out whose fault.

Blame is powerless. Because it is punitive, negative, evasive, blaming tends to merely increase the inner frustrations and conflicts in both parties which contributed to the original breakdown in communication or relationship. This leads to cyclical criticisms of each other whether expressed in words or acted out in silence or submission.

One. When two people get stuck in a blaming dance (each blames the other, neither can let go), assigning ratios of responsibility is useless. Both are partly right, partly wrong.

Two. When one person gets into blaming, the recipient can express regrets for any actual behavior and offer an appropriate change. If the blaming continues, further justifying or returning the blame only provokes more unreasonable words.

Three. When blaming goes beyond shaming to attempt to hook another's guilt, it only succeeds where there is guilt available to be hooked. As one makes peace with old guilt residues and lives in responsibility thinking, then the hook is cast in vain. The blamed will not blame the blamer for blaming, and the cycle ends.[5]

The goal is to return to responsibility thinking as quickly as possible when either feeling the impulse to blame or to react to blame. Ask, "What response did I actually make or fail to make which helped trigger this incident?" If you can identify either, then the ability to respond further or in new ways will be present. If you were not at all involved, then the ability to be empathetic is the response-ability that leads to healing.

Dirty Fighting Code

Leap to the offense when feeling offended. The blame is going to land somewhere; be first to label it, place it, prove it and you are off the hook, off the carpet, out of the bind.

Fair Fighting Creed

"I am always responsible for whatever I do, think, feel, choose. I am never to blame. I am not available for blame, activated by blame, aroused by blame. You are always responsible, you are never to blame."

Exercises

1. Discuss the three options given for blaming cycles with a fellow struggler in the blaming dance. Can you make a decision to take a small step toward forgetting whose fault and instead choosing whose move it is?
2. Set the rumor afloat in your own unconscious that you are not to blame (negative), you are responsible (positive). Seek to internalize the fair fighting creed by discussing it with another person with whom you have been hooked in the past.

Day Fifteen
Who's Right?

Old Self Instructions

Find who's right

Keep the focus clean,
clear.
Keep the issues sharp,
simple.
Either/or, right/wrong
True/false, Nice/nasty.
Some people are wrong
(like you, no offense
intended).
Some people are right
(like me, how can I
help it?).
Admit it, face it, let's get
on with it.

New Self Instructions

Find what's right

The central issue is . . .
Not who, but what,
Not which one of us
But which way for us.
My perspective is not
"right,"
Nor your point of view
"wrong."
Each is partial, personal,
private.
Each is corrected,
completed, clarified
By hearing, valuing,
gaining from
the other.

"I happen to be right, you happen to be wrong, why must you close your eyes to the obvious?"
(there are only two kinds of people in the world, the right and the wrong, the good and the bad)

"The issue is not what you feel or not even what you think, but what really happened."
(and which of us can go beyond our thoughts and feelings to speak for "reality")

"If you'd only listen to reason, we wouldn't have these differences over what is so patently clear!"
(reason may be final for the rational, understanding is fundamental for the emotional, compassion is crucial for the relational)

For some battlers, truth is the bottom line in any conflict. The obsession with getting to the root of any issue, holding out for the last word, discovering the absolute cause drives a tough battler to fight until the last *T* is crossed in his way, last *I* dotted in her way.

In stress, most persons find their thinking becomes more concrete, alternatives become more simple. People appear to be either for or against us, their motives either good or evil, and the issues more and more clearly right or wrong.

In stress, we regress to concrete thinking with amazing speed. The old two-part categories of either/or, nice/nasty, good/evil are used to stamp persons or problems as right/wrong, true/false with deceptive simplicity. These concrete thinking patterns which easily separate the bad guys from the good gals emerge in childhood, and remain as a basic kind of emotional thought even though maturity provides more accurate and diverse ways of seeing all the variety within reality.

In threatening situations the temptation to see the world in we/they terms reaches far back to the fears and insecurities of our helpless years. "We" are trustworthy, "they" are threatening, "we" are safe, "they" are dangerous, "we" are family and friends, "they" are foes and enemies. The trap hidden in this adversary thinking is treacherous since "we" are invariably on the side of truth, justice, privilege and "they" deserve whatever we are giving them. The we/they division can support male or female sexism, ageism, racism, ethnic prejudice, and nationalism. Only when we begin to understand that there is good and bad on both sides of any issue, in both camps of any conflict, are we able to bridge differences and connect with others.

Distrust all we/they divisions. We are all more similar than different. And conflict is caused less by our differences than by our similarities. Differences may be the occasion, similarities are more often the cause of hassles. When I observe a fault in you that irritates me, there is every likelihood that your fault is my fault too. If I am at peace within myself with the behavior in question, then I will feel sympathy, sadness, or support for you even as I may choose to disagree or object without rancor.

Suspect all concrete categories. "There are only two kinds of people in this world," some philosopher has suggested, "those who think there are two kinds, and those who think there are more." There are so many variations both within and between persons that categories, cubbyholes, and labels are of limited, temporary use. Once the other person is known more deeply, the old descriptions fold and fail.

Forget which one of us is right, which wrong. The truth is always greater than either side's point of view. The issue is not who is right but what is right. Each point of view is partial, personal, private. No human perspective embraces the whole. Each person in a relationship is completed, corrected, clarified by the other. To join in seeking joint perceptions, shared understandings, mutual recognition of what is right leads to a sense of togetherness with integrity.

The defensiveness which needs to be right, or more often needs to be seen as right, is a competitive drive to be one up. When one feels an inner demand that "nothing is settled until I say it's settled, nothing is right until I hear you say that I am right," then the need to win and the need to see the other lose must both be ended.

Dirty Fighting Code

"I have the last word, you must hear it; I will win the last round, you will lose it. Right is right, wrong is wrong. Face it, admit it, accept it."

Fair Fighting Creed

"Your truth, my truth, our truth are all part truths. The humility to confess my fallibility while asserting my full ability allows us to both respect and correct each other."

Exercises

1. Choose the person you like least. List the ways you differ. Then note the ways you are alike. Which list is more volatile in igniting conflict?
2. Reflect on those situations in which you become intensely concerned to prove yourself right, the other wrong. Identify the fears that are attached to being proved wrong.
3. Review a situation more than a month old in which you insisted on being right. In hindsight, reassess your "rightness." Now that it's past, note how more tentative the feelings are today.

Day Sixteen
Walking Out

Old Self Instructions

Walk out, clam up, shut off

Clam up when cornered.
Cut off a losing argument.
Get out of tense situations.
Send off the kids to their rooms.
Shut out unpleasant facts.
Lay off difficult employees.
Turn in your resignation when stressed.
Claim the way of escape.

New Self Instructions

Work through to break through

I will differ without withdrawing.
I will disagree without distancing.
I will care and confront without fleeing or facade.
I will work through until we break through.

"I just take it, quietly. I've nothing to say, talking only makes it worse."
(passive withdrawal from hopeless feelings)

"I just ignore her when she gets upset and that really gets her, she can't do anything about it!"
(passive aggression from angry feelings)

"I just get away as quickly as I can. I can't stand conflict. I get all panicky inside. I have to get away."
(passive flight from helpless feelings)

"I quit. When things aren't going the way I think they should, count me out. I resign."
(active flight as a power play)

Hopelessness, helplessness, or pessimism is the central feeling behind the great strategy of walking out. From the passive style of blending into the wallpaper to the deliberate and defiant choice to stonewall another with angry silence, the "walk-out, clam-up, shut-off" style of fighting has more variations than any other conflict response. It should, since it is the most widely used conflict behavior, according to all published test results. When tension rises, the majority of persons either leave the conflict psychologically or look for the exit physically.

Helplessness is the most common feeling. The expectation of losing is so overwhelming that the person simply opts out of the situation. "Why get caught up in endless struggles which can only lead to another painful failure? Better to get out with a small loss of face than to be totally devastated!"

Hopelessness is the other twin emotion. "Since people are concerned only about themselves and their own needs, conflict is a hopeless situation. The enlightened response is to just patiently step back, stay uninvolved, let it run its course without you. Getting involved only leads to ongoing hostilities and unresolvable binds that are worse than those at the outset."

Pessimism is the solution. "Nothing good can come of open disagreement. Silence is the only eloquent response, avoidance is the only wise strategy, distance the only safe place."

The range of behaviors that follow offers something for everyone. The workaholic can bury himself in his work, or drive herself mercilessly in her career to be unavailable. The sports enthusiast can keep on the move to stay out of reach. The spectators on life can hide in the paper, attach themselves to the television, remain a voyeur on real human contact.

The key element in all of these is escape, flight, seeking an exit. It is a deliberate choice to lose now by leaving the field rather than risk a greater loss by entering negotiation. But an escape from conflict is also an exit from intimacy. The closeness that triggers the impulse to rework a relationship is the same closeness that meets our human needs for contact and caring. We all have differing needs for distance, and the one who can tolerate most may use that edge to manipulate the other in a relationship. Withdrawing threatens rejection. Distancing invites pursuit. Flight stimulates the fear of losing the relationship. So the manipulative power of losing in order to win by intimidation or alienation is attractive to the persons who allow themselves to be aggressive only in passive ways. Walking out symbolizes the end of the relationship. Clamming up announces the coldness of a friendship in winter. Cutting off contact in any way warns of impending separation.

The tensions between union and separation are among the most basic feelings felt lifelong. Love is a creative balance between union and separation. Too close a union can swallow up one or stifle both. Too great a separation can sever the relationship. To threaten the basic understanding of ongoing association cuts at the bottom line of a relationship. Thus nothing scares more deeply, angers more thoroughly, frustrates more completely than any form of walking out.

The basic ground upon which conflict management depends is a commitment to continuing relationship. There must be a primary earnestness about ongoing trust and long-term openness to creative association. When such primary understandings exist, secondary issues can be worked through to the advantage of both.

This is why withdrawal is so powerful, so commonly used, and so destructive. To threaten the basic floor of human trust is to undermine the ground on which we both stand.

Maturity is shown best by an individual's ability to differ without immediate distancing, to disagree without withdrawing. Genuine adulthood is demonstrated by the capacity to offer warm caring and firm confrontation without hiding behind a facade or fleeing into covert strategies.

Presence, not absence, is the real source of power. And an act of will is the answer—"I will work through until we break through; I'm here to stay."

Dirty Fighting Code

When in threat, walk out. When in doubt, clam up. When in trouble, get out. When resentful, shut others out. Exit is the word.

Fair Fighting Creed

"I will stand with you, struggle with you, strike new agreements with you as long as it is productive for us both."

Exercises

1. Helplessness: Conflict triggers helpless feelings in any aware person. Can you recognize these in yourself? Can you admit them to others? Can you, along with the helplessness, find the commitment to keep working? Share your experience of this balance of weakness and strength with another person.
2. Hopelessness: Be aware of the depressive core of hopeless feelings that wells up when conflict seems to promise nothing. Identify those hopes which should die. Focus on those hopes that can endure.
3. Pessimism: For every pessimistic thought there is an opposite with more optimistic promise. Both are partly true. Can you believe both? Pick a situation you find discouraging. List three reasons for new courage.

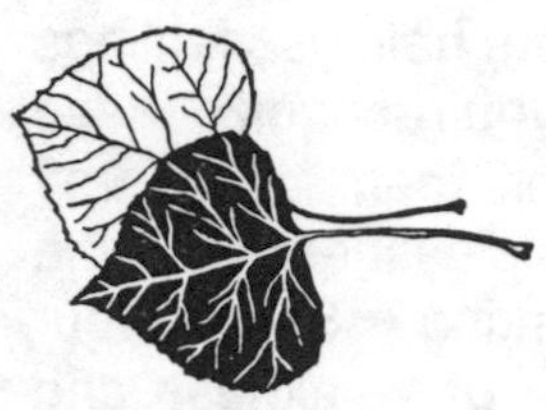

Day Seventeen

Joking

Old Self Instructions

Use sarcasm

Soften the other with a smile
Then slip in the steel of irony.
Cover the chill of icy wit
With false but friendly warmth.
Jab with a jest, but lightly.
It's nothing more than a joke.
Save your best sarcasm
For when you have an audience.

New Self Instructions

Delight in humor

I will recognize that the line
Between tragedy and comedy is thin
(my, your, our immaturity is both).
I will smile at our hassles
Which I once saw as tragic.
I will chuckle at our cycles
Which I once saw as catastrophic.
I am free as I can see my folly.

"When you say that, you better smile!"
(the chill of wit needs human warmth)

"So the world is all wrong and you're all right?"
(one line of humor can carry hostility, rejection, judgment, condemnation, and deliver them all)

"What is funny when I say it to you, is not at all funny when you say it to me."
(one man's humorous attempt is another's contempt)

The most devastating remarks can be dropped in jest. If the other takes offense, you can tease him or her about being too sensitive. If s/he ignores it, you can note what thick skin s/he has. The art of putting the other's feet to the fire is to do it so warmly that s/he will not know s/he has been burned until the conversation is over.

If an attack is to be made, do it with sarcasm, but smile to show it is all in good fun. If you can pull it off in public it will demonstrate what a delightful fun-loving person you are in contrast to the other who is an irritable clod with no sense of humor.

Recognize these strategies? The humorous ambush can trip up the other when off guard, then cover with the guise of easy laughter. As a clever conflict dance, it can keep persons sparring indefinitely.

The greatest loss in such binds is that humor, the sign of healing, is used to hurt another. Laughter, the signal of tension release, the sound of celebration, the sign of joyful acceptance may be used for the exact opposite—tension creation, alienation, rejection.

When two people fighting can laugh benevolently at each other, chuckle acceptantly at the other's way of scoring points, or joke at his or her own discomfort, it draws the sting out of threatening situations and draws the two closer together.

When, however, one gets sarcastic delight from another's discomfort, or enjoys the embarrassment that follows a touch of ridicule, or if one clowns, spoofs or gives flip replies to another's seriousness, then the two are separated, even estranged by the uses of humor.

Clean humor is bonding. When two persons in conflict can smile at themselves and each other safely, unashamedly, taking each other's teasing in good grace with no loss of face, then the humor connects them at a playful level even while serious work is being done. The laughter is a signal that the foundational relationship of good will is holding firm while the surface is getting rearranged or redesigned. They can actually be kids together once more as they mimic their own or the other's faults and put down the pretenses that complicate their lives.

Cutting humor is surgical and separating. It bites deeply into self-esteem, pokes sharply at appearance, performance, or personality. Its negative power lies in its hidden judgments, devaluations, and the subtle ways it can dehumanize.

The gift of humor is the ability to see the saving grace of comedy in what was previously experienced as tragedy. The line between tragedy and comedy is so thin because the identical data between two persons can be viewed with extreme sadness or exhilarating mirth.

"Suffering too is funny" is an ancient Hebrew proverb from the learnings of an abused people. When one can no longer laugh at the difficulties of life, one is ceasing to live. And these further words of Jewish wisdom: "There are three things which are real: God, human folly, and laughter. The first two are beyond our comprehension. So we must do what we can with the third."

In each of us there is both a wise person and a fool. We must learn to love the fool within—the character who swings too widely in exaggerated feelings, then over-talks, overreacts, overdoes it. If I can love my fool and you can love yours, I'll be able to chuckle when you point out mine and you may be able to smile when I notice yours. It is the fool within that humanizes my inner tyrant and suggests some much needed humility. Accepting both sides as necessary for wholeness allows us to quit taking life and relationships with exaggerated seriousness, and to begin working seriously at some much needed frivolity.

Freedom from old binds is becoming real when one can smile at hassles which once seemed calamitous, or chuckle at old negative cycles which once felt catastrophic. To be able to relax and join in the other's laughter, even when it begins a bit before one is ready to chuckle about the self, can move a conflict toward resolution. Smile. There's freedom within it.

Dirty Fighting Code

"I will needle you with wit, salt our conflict with sarcasm, soften you with humor to nudge you into seeing, thinking, acting in my way."

Fair Fighting Creed

"I will laugh with you, not at you; I will join you in your humor, not fight it. Love me, love my fool. I will learn to love you, wise, fool, and all."

Exercises

1. Recall tense areas of guilt or shame felt in your

family of origin. Have you been able to laugh at them? When was the first time you could see them with humor?

2. Choose a painful failure from your life that you have frequently recalled with pain or embarrassment. Tell it in tragic terms. Observe the feelings stimulated. Now retell the same events as a comedy. Can you smile at the event once seen as tragic?
3. Reflect on the different emotional feelings that emerge from humor that belittles and humor that liberates!

Day Eighteen
Questioning

Old Self Instructions

Use clever questions

Leading questions
seduce.
Punishing questions
ridicule.
Set-up questions
manipulate.
Trapping questions bind.
Commanding questions
order.
Hypothetical questions
criticize,
(And they are clever,
concealed,
hidden.)

New Self Instructions

Make clear statements

I will make clear
statements,
I will welcome yours.
I will make frank
requests,
I will honor yours.
I will give simple
invitations,
I will respect yours.
(And they're single level,
and open.)

"Don't you think that . . . "
(if you thought it, you'd have said it; I think it and want to lead you to it)

"Why did you spill the milk on the carpet?"
(I'm not interested in your reasons; I simply want to tell you they are lousy reasons)

"When are you going to do something about . . . "
(a concealed command that "is only a question")

"Didn't you once say that . . . "
(maneuvers the other into a vulnerable or a compromising position)

The most frequently misused communication pattern is the question. Few questions asked in times of stress serve to clarify confusion, in fact they more often increase it.

When pressed by the stress of conflict, questions spring up as a natural defense. And they pass for communication even though they transmit emotion with little information.

"Why did you walk out last night without saying a word?"

"Do you really want to know?"

"If I didn't, would I ask?"

"If you ask, does that prove you care?"

"Why do you question everything I say?"

"Don't you realize that you ask as many questions as I do?"

Two questioners are passing each other by. Each question conceals a comment that could bring them into communication, yet they dance around the question marks, dangling them like fishhooks to snare the other's feelings. So they slip judgments, criticisms, punishments, come-ons into an innocent series of questions.[6]

The leading question is a come-on for getting the other person to say what you want him or her to say. "Wouldn't you say that it's better to . . . "

The punishing question is a put-down, a criticism, a censure, a sly stroke of ridicule. "Why did you try to beat the light when you know the police are arresting on yellow?" "What makes you think you can get away with that?"

The trapping question is a setup that snookers the other in a vulnerable spot where s/he can be "had." "Isn't it true that you promised to never . . . "

The avoiding question is a runaround multiple choice item which can mean anything either might want it to mean. "What do you want to do tonight?" "Why don't you choose?" "What are you waiting for?" "What do you mean by that?"

The commanding question is a covert demand made as an innocent question. If the other resists one can insist, "What's wrong with asking?" Examples are, "When are you going to do something about . . . ?" "Why don't you get started on . . . ?"

All of these are closed questions which limit the possible responses of the other and reduce the freedom to respond fully. These closed questions trap, enmesh, entangle persons with each other so that little information is exchanged, and emotions are inflamed.

Open-ended questions are single level. They make direct requests for repetition, clarification, or further information. Open-ended questions invite the other to think more freely, answer more broadly, communicate more fully.

Even more effective is the intentional use of invitations and statements to replace questions. A clear statement of interest, curiosity, puzzlement invites the other to share his or her preference or thoughts.

"Tell me what you prefer."

"I'd like to hear your view."

"I'm curious about your feelings toward . . ."

The most powerful form of communication is the invitation. As persons offer each other open-ended questions, clear statements, and warm invitations, they can move past defensiveness to truly hear the other's meanings.

As soon as conflict rises, discard questions and return to statements and invitations. The moment tensions rise, questions become too slippery to carry the needed data or the real emotions.

Dirty Fighting Code

Stay just out of reach. Lead, set up, trap, command, punish in subtle disguise by asking questions, just questions, innocent questions!

Fair Fighting Creed

"I will say what I want, I think, I choose, I value in single level, open-ended statements and invitations."

Exercises

1. Reflect on a recent conflict. Can you recall more statements made to you, or questions asked of you? Note whether you can now list more unanswered questions you would like to ask or statements you wish to make?
2. With a friend or spouse, communicate (or miscommunicate) for three minutes using all five kinds of questions described here. Then debrief your awareness of how you use questions to shield, screen, hide, or control others.

Day Nineteen
Triangling

Old Self Instructions

Pit people against people

Quote others freely
(to prove your points).
Use others gladly
(to carry your
messages).
Pit others against others
(to prod, or bind).
Compare others with
others
(to motivate or deflate).
Refer to those not
present
(as the final court or
authority).
Go through, over, around,
under
anyone you can,
anything you can.

New Self Instructions

Deal only firsthand

I will say
What I have to say
without citing others,
without using others,
without triangling
others,
Without involving others
as judge
as witness
as expert
as jury.
I will deal with you
one-to-one,
face-to-face,
person-to-person.

"You're alright, you know. I don't care what all the others said about you!"
(beware of hidden triangles)

"If you knew what your brother said about you. Well, you might as well hear it now."
(be wary of triangling people)

"I'm amazed at your offer; I'm much more impressed with your partner's estimate."
(be aware of your own impulses to pit people against people)

Dysfunctional relationships tend to be triangular. It takes three to tangle. In stress, the most anxious party in a difference will bring in a third person to reduce the inner tension.[7]

The process is sinfully simple. Pit others against each other. "Let you and him fight rather than you and me." The triangular lines bring back memories of childhood to most of us. "You just wait until your father gets home." (The fear is now between child and father.) "I just hope your mother never finds out what you did, it would break her heart." (Now the anxiety is reduced in the father since it is raised between child and mother.) "Tommy always gets all the breaks, you like him better than me." (Triangling a sibling to hook parental guilt spreads the pain around.)

Triangling begins early. When two people discover that they are not effective lovers and their marriage is in difficulty, the common solution is to turn themselves into parents. Already during pregnancy the child becomes a buffer, a third party who absorbs the thinking and feeling time and energies of both. Unless the parental coalition is reaffirmed, so that the two adults are lovers first and parents second, the triangle will continue.

Effective conflict resolution is invariably a two-person process. In a dyad, the two can dialogue until a balanced solution emerges. In a triad, there is always a close pair and an outside third person. The dysfunctions emerge as responsibility gets laid on the outside but innocent third person, or the relationships rotate and now you're close to one, now the other, now distant from both.

Pitting persons against each other makes resolution impossible. When a child is triangled between parents there is no freedom for anyone to relate honestly. When a third party is drawn into a marriage in an affair, everyone loses. When an absent person is quoted as criticizing another to prove your own objections, there is no effective conclusion.

The pain rises from passing messages around the triangle, passing tensions from person to person, pitting the strengths of one against the weaknesses of the other.

The art of triangling is second nature to anyone who grew up in the human family. (It has a long history. Eve—snake—God, Eve—snake—Adam, Adam—Eve—God, etc. Note how the responsibility got circulated in the earliest conflict account.) The skills are virtually automatic.

Quote others freely to prove a crucial point (and pass off the present anxiety to that absent relationship).

Use others gladly to carry your messages (and be snookered into the responsibility for their contents).

Compare others with others to motivate or deflate (and stir up tensions between them that you can control).

Refer to those not present as the final authority on anything (then you cannot be challenged or disproved).

All of these strategies are means of going over, through, under, around others rather than working out differences *with* them.

The alternative is to build genuine one-to-one relationships, to say what needs to be said directly, levelly, without any use of people not present. Set the third party free to truly be outside, unhooked, unentangled. Deal only face-to-face, one-to-one, person-to-person.

Dirty Fighting Code

Never enter a conflict alone. Always use a quotation, an irritation, a competition, an unequal comparison, another relationship to pry the other off balance, nudge him off center, get her off your case.

Fair Fighting Creed

"I will say what I have to say to you, work out what I have to work out with you, resolve what I need to resolve with you."

Exercises

1. Since families are collections of triangles (one child, one triangle; two children, four triangles; three children, ten triangles), reflect on which triangle was the most painful for you. How did you learn to quickly move to the safer outside position and pass off the tension to a third?
2. Reflect on those situations in which you now feel triangled—with parents, siblings, spouse, coworkers. How can you reclaim the conflict and deal with it in dialogue?
3. Make a list of the triangular strategies you are

skilled at using to dissipate a conflict. Can you identify why they are powerless, dysfunctional, destructive. Plan constructive one-to-one behaviors for the future.

Day Twenty
Undermining

Old Self Instructions

Undermine self-esteem

Deflate self-respect.
Undermine self-confidence.
Reduce independence.
Decrease autonomy.
Impugn motives.
Chip away self-esteem.
Remember vulnerable points
for future use if necessary.

New Self Instructions

Enrich self-esteem

I will disconnect . . .
self-esteem from success,
self-respect from failure,
self-worth from performance,
self-regard from competition,
self-confidence from appearance.
My worth is not increased by winning,
Your worth is not insured by being right.
Nothing can increase or reduce it.

"Winning isn't everything, it's the only thing. Winners are the whole show, losers are forgotten."
(when worth and success get connected, both fail)

"When I am doing well, I feel great about myself. When things are not going well, I feel lousy."
(when self-esteem gets connected to performance, neither can survive the test)

"What kind of person are you, anyway? How could you have done this to me?"
(when self-esteem is attacked, when basic worth gets undermined, all else is up for grabs)

To wipe out the opposition, attack self-esteem; to take the wind out of their sails, reduce their self-worth; to eliminate their will to win, challenge their self-confidence; to drive them back to their basic survival responses, attack their right to be.

These ways of undermining the opponent's basic ground come naturally to those for whom winning is everything. Once their self-respect is attached to their success, they expect it in others, and can zero in to torpedo the core self-esteem of the other person with deadly accuracy.

The problem for the attacker and the attacked lies in the absence of a real center. When appearance, compliance, and performance remain as the ongoing center of a person, he or she is crucially vulnerable at the very core. In early childhood, one has only a knowledge of secondary self-esteem based on one's achievement and conformity on the acceptance and approval won. Gradually one separates core valuations of the self and internalizes these messages as an enduring center of self-worth. Personhood emerges as one can perceive that every human being is a center of created worth that can neither be increased nor decreased by performance. We are each irreducibly valuable. Nothing one does or does not do can reduce that person's worth, nothing can increase it. Each is a being to be prized simply for being.

Thus there are two levels of self-esteem: (1) core self-esteem which is both recognized as a given in our creation and internalized from the love and acceptance of those around us; (2) performance esteem which rises from our day-to-day assessment of behavioral success. Maturity is being able to go on feeling good about oneself even when not feeling good about a particular behavior or venture or relationship.

When success is the center of a person's worth, the person has no center. Success is always relative, conditional, temporary, vulnerable, here today but unsure tomorrow. Success, achievement, performance are all out there, not in here. One must go on succeeding, continue performing, or the worth evaporates.

Two central commitments can honor self-esteem in situations of stress or distress.

One, a commitment to yourself to disconnect self-esteem from success or failure, from performance or competition, from appearance or approval. All of these are important, even crucial to your day-to-day feelings about your life, but they dare not dictate your feelings about your self. You are worthful no matter what kind of situation you are in at the moment. The union between worth and performance is a learned condition, and it can be unlearned.

Two, a commitment to others to see them as worthful apart from their behavior. No matter how down you may be on another's performance, their personhood and personal value can be prized even as the confrontation is being made. This concern for others disarms one of any right to attack the person, but rather than reducing the power of confrontation it increases it. Any disagreement that rejects the whole person is powerless to invite change. Only when one knows that personhood is safe can change in behavior be freely envisioned and ventured.

Maintaining a core of calm in the midst of conflict requires a constant practice of disconnecting any of the old connections between internal values and external verdicts on current achievements. The way to insure that your own old connections are severed is to assure others that their self-esteem is safe with you, their self-respect will not be questioned.

People are precious, worthful, simply because they are, not because they are as you or I prefer or prescribe. To honor that, is to prize the neighbor as you prize yourself.

Dirty Fighting Code

When threatened, go for the gut, deflate self-respect; go for the throat, reduce self-esteem.

Fair Fighting Creed

"Each person's autonomy, independence, integrity as a worthful valuable human is sacred. I will honor it as I honor my own."

Exercises

To disconnect self-esteem from performance esteem, reflect on the following affirmations . . .

1. I am the thinker, not the thought, so I am worthful no matter what painful thoughts. I am free to think new thoughts.
2. I am the feeler, not the feeling, so I am precious

no matter what hurtful feelings. I am free to change and grow.

3. I am the doer, not the deed, so I am valuable no matter what my actions. I am free to behave in more useful ways.
4. I am the performer, not the performance, so I am I no matter how well I do. I am free to try again.

Day Twenty-One
Martyrdom

Old Self Instructions

Be a martyr (or saint)

Sacrifice, yield,
surrender,
Comply, kowtow, submit.
Give in with longsuffering
saintliness,
Give up with righteous
superiority.
Never use obvious power
When guilt and shame
are available.
The sighing martyr is
dynamic.
The silent martyr is
dynamite.

New Self Instructions

Be equal, mutual

I will stand equal
without placating.
I will stand mutual
without ingratiating.
I will stand level
without groveling.
I will neither use or be
used,
I will never abuse nor be
abused.

"You just go on and have a good time; I'll stay home alone here and get the work done. Don't give it a thought."
(the sigh of the martyr is heard again)

"You're probably right, I was out of place to object. I'm deeply sorry."
(the apology of the martyr is heard again)

"It's no problem, no, you are not taking advantage of me. It's quite all right."
(the groveling of a martyr is seen again)

The impulse to suffer is an amazing trait among human beings. The willingness to absorb hostility warmly, bear injustice gladly, accept abuse freely rises from a vision of the self as sacrifice, a vision often learned so early and buried so deeply that it is beneath awareness. A true martyr will deny that there was any sacrifice involved. "Someone has to do it, it was nothing, don't give it a second thought."

The power of the martyr is the power of guilt. Subtle, hidden, covert, yet potent, it works the long slow change created by inner discomfort. The victim has equal power with the victimizer, and since it takes longer, the victim more often has the last word. The top dog may growl and bite, but the underdog wins in the end. Covert power reaches more deeply than the obvious, overt powers.

The sighing martyr finds a way to communicate the suffering felt without ever putting it into words. The pained expression, the grieved attitude, the hurt look all do their slow work on the other person's conscience. Slowly the sighs mount up to an inaudible roar and the other pays off in some contrite or begrudging way.

The silent martyr is even more dynamic; in fact, dynamite. The long practice of absorbing the pain in the relationship can earn a place of unacknowledged power. The scapegoat in a family is usually the last to be willing for change to come. The victim hesitates to give up the role and the influence it really has on the whole family system.

The righteous martyr has the additional blessing of invisible superiority. While sacrificing joyfully for the sake of others, the unselfishness is so clearly demonstrated the person need never say, "See how little I demand for myself, how I always put others first, how calmly I bear up under injustice." The unselfish person can be incredibly self-righteous, and invisibly so.

Martyrdom before the repeated tyranny of a persecutor only continues the cycle. Victim and victimizer are two halves of the same whole. If one plays victim it builds the rage in the other which will lead to ongoing repetitions of the drama. Only when both sides are present in each person does the balancing integration occur which can heal the empty hurt in both.

Placating the blamer is a temporary solution since it fuels the anger and resentment in the blamer which ultimately invites more of the same.

Groveling before a punishing judge only insures that the two will dance this dance again. Even as the obsequious words are being said, the resistance is building in both that will emerge again in another round of the same mismatch.

Saccharine sainthood only exaggerates the sinfulness of the partner. When one takes the polar role of saint, the other must either be absorbed into the same perfection or take the opposite pole of sinner. Many partners find themselves caught in these two-part dramas—erring husband, forgiving wife, or virtuous husband, adventuring wife.

Healing, growth, and fulfillment in relationship depend on mutuality. Only as each determines within the self to stand equal without placating or blaming; to stand parallel without scolding or ingratiating; to stand level without condemning or groveling, can negative cycles be broken. It takes two to continue these old cycles, it takes one to quit.

Dirty Fighting Code

Never speak when a sign will suffice, never stand up when groveling will do, never complain when silence will salt the wound. Trust the power of guilt.

Fair Fighting Creed

Stand level, neither move over nor under the other. Stand equal, neither act superior nor inferior to the other. Stand mutual, neither claim too much nor too little responsibility in relationship.

Exercises

Finish each of the following lines in at least three ways.

1. "When I give another the silent treatment, I am expecting . . ."
2. "When I obviously do much more than my share of the junk work, my hope is . . ."
3. While pole of each of these pairs do you find more fitting to your personality: Placater/Blamer? Martyr/Persecutor? Judge/Groveler? Saint/Sinner? How do you invite another into the interaction? How can you call off the game?

Day Twenty-Two
Controlling

Old Self Instructions

Threatening, binding, manipulating

If I find what you fear
I can threaten those
fears.
If I learn what you hate
I can play on your
dislikes.
If I know what you love
I can threaten its loss.
So I can coerce, seduce,
control,
If you give me the power
to push
and pull.

New Self Instructions

Freeing

I am free to share my
fears,
I will not meddle in
yours.
I am free to express my
tastes and likes,
I will not manipulate
yours.
I am free to affirm my
values,
I will not endanger
yours.
I will seek only to control
My half of our
relationship.

"Hold it right there. This has got to stop. I am outraged that you would go over my head like that. It better never happen again."
(controlling-anger is coercion)

"How could you do that to me, after all I've done for you? At least you could show some gratitude that I've never asked you to be grateful.
(controlling-guilt is blackmail)

"If you loved me, you wouldn't think of getting involved in that, no matter how attractive it may be."
(controlling-love is manipulation)

The need to control is one of the most common relationship killers that we humans mistakenly use as a cure. As with many toxic substances, a measured amount can be beneficial, but more of a good thing is rarely better, and exercising more than carefully limited control is fatal to loving relationships.

The controlling personality hates surprises, dislikes spontaneity, and prefers to blueprint life to eliminate the unpredictable. He wants to program people or events. She wants to eliminate differences that do not fit into her range of acceptable behavior for herself. He is threatened by independent, autonomous people who do not have completely predictable "character." She tries constantly to control others' feelings toward her, and then doubts their sincerity when they are exactly what she was demanding.

The need for control manifests itself as a desire for power, authority, dominance over others and therefore over one's future. Behind the need lurk fears—fears of powerlessness and helplessness, fears of being controlled and betrayed, fears of being dominated and used. The need to be in control indicates that there is a failure of primary trust for others in the personality. The fundamental impulse is to have complete mastery over another person or the whole life situation. The significant people cannot be trusted to become free and independent and cease to be possessed, so domination is attempted by outright exercise of power or by indirect manipulation of shame, guilt, or love.

Whenever you are motivated by a need to control others, you are likely to use one of four basic weapons: anger, guilt, love, or law.

Controlling with anger and irritation is a coercive method of overpowering the other person with emotional demands. If I find out what you fear, I can threaten those fears with my rage or subtly undermine them with my malice. For parents, the threat may be to withdraw love and security, to abandon, to punish. For partners, the threat may be to withhold affection or to leave. With associates it may be to cut off the friendship, terminate the working relationship, or simply make life difficult. All are means of coercive control.

Controlling with guilt and shame is an invasion of the other person's emotional world to blackmail him into complying. When one induces pity, shame or guilt, one is blaming the other for neglecting, hurting, betraying, not living up to the controller's legitimate needs. "You're breaking my heart, shortening my life, making me unhappy, giving me a heart attack." And at its best it threatens suicide.

Controlling with "love and affection" includes manipulative strategies of appeasing, placating, seducing, spoiling with kindness, brainwashing, snuggling up like a child demanding care, surrounding and smothering with "loving care" like a compulsive parent. "I'm sorry, I didn't mean to hurt you (now join me in feeling guilty about this hassle)." "I really like you, I'll always be on your side defending you (and you better reciprocate)." "Let me help you, protect you, take care of you (and let me lean on you)."

Controlling with rules and law calls down the external authorities of legality, convention, tradition to authorize the programming of the other person according to the controller's prescriptions. "It just isn't done that way." "Sorry, but the rule prohibits it." By calling in the structures of those rules that meet one's own ends, the other can be shaped in desired ways.

Controlling behavior is invariably self-defeating. Effective parenting seeks to work itself out of the job of controlling as rapidly as the child can assume it responsibly. Turning over the control and direction of its own life to the child happens in a small part the first day (cry if you feel pain) and increases throughout life until identity and responsibility find their center in adolescence and youth.

Creative marriage grows as both partners recognize that control of the other is not only nonproductive, it is undesirable. Control is the antithesis of love since the more I love you, the more I set you free.

Constructive living, working and befriending respects the other person's integrity as an active, autonomous agent of choice and change. Persons change slowly and from within. The imposition of external controls is temporary and, in emergency, only briefly helpful at best. The loving response is to return responsibility to the other as soon as possible. Internalized controls, inner direction, centered identity, and responsibility are the goals of maturity. My own maturity is shown by my ability to foster these in the lives of those who are near and dear to me.

Dirty Fighting Code

To be safe, take control. To be sure, run it yourself. To be secure, claim both the power and the authority to dictate what is best for all.

Fair Fighting Creed

"I will share my weakness and my strength, my fears and my faith, my anxiety and my calm. I will not pretend the one and deny the other. I will not seek to reduce the one by dominating with the other."

Exercises

To identify your need to be in control, watch for these patterns:

1. Are you irritated by daily events and often think of changing them?
2. Do you find others' expressions of feelings, frustrations, actions often are intolerable and you wish you could help rework them?
3. Are you repelled by parts of others' self-presentation—dress, talk, laughter, seductiveness, friendliness?
4. Do you often feel judgmental of others' lifestyles as too conforming? Too nonconformist? Too different?
5. Do you seek to influence others' choices and actions to your better way? Do you seek to persuade others to do things in the way you want them done?
6. Do you feel that since someone has to take charge, you need to see after most things or they do not get done?

Reflect on what would happen to others, to you, to your relationship if you discontinued any or all of the above.

Day Twenty-Three
Delaying

Old Self Instructions	**New Self Instructions**
Ignore, forget, postpone	***Contract, commit covenant***
Overlook expectations (they limit).	Commit!
Forget agreements (they block).	Life is promise. Risk!
Avoid promises (they trap).	Contract!
Postpone obligations (they bind).	Life is keeping faith.
Delay commitments (they kill).	Trust!
Tomorrow.	Covenant!
	Life is loving faithfully.
	Love!

"Frankly, it just slipped my mind, besides, it wasn't all that important anyway so why be upset?"
(chronic forgetting can get a lot of frustration expressed)

"I'll get at it tomorrow, there's no rush as I see it, so relax. I said I'd do it, didn't I?"
(chronic postponing can get a great deal of irritation out)

"I just didn't notice, I've a lot on my mind these days so it just slipped past me."
(convenient ignoring can delay, derail, deflect problems that deserve resolution)

The Chinese invented the classic water torture techniques that slowly, drop by drop, drive the victim to the blessed relief of insanity. But they are not alone in knowing how little betrayals, small deceptions, daily failures to keep promises, can be crazy-making. The arts of getting even by postponing, getting back at another by forgetting an agreement, or getting satisfaction out of ignoring another during difficulty, are universal human means of passive aggression.

"Don't get mad, get even" is a silent strategy often practiced by very "good" people who balance off their feeling ledgers by the innocent means of dragging their feet, overbooking their schedules, overextending themselves elsewhere. Like the proverbial waiter who spits in the soup of the nasty customer and then serves it with a smile, they can get at the other without being gotten.

Forgetting is such an excusable way to resist authorities, frustrate friends, spite a spouse. "I forgot," is a wonderful all-purpose excuse from early childhood when it represented the only power often available to a small tot in the land of giants.

Done intentionally, the forgetter never keeps a promise, neglects to do an errand, doesn't recall a requested favor, can't remember an obligation to another. Then the forgetter can act surprised, even shocked, when the other gets upset. "How unreasonable to be angry when I simply forgot," as if to imply that it was not that important anyway.

Postponing is an even more effective way to keep the other on tenterhooks. Delaying carrying out promises or obligations can slowly raise the stress in another while the eleventh hour approaches. Stalling on a necessary task can get to the other, the more their work or responsibility depends on it the better. When the complaints are tendered, one can be sweetly reassuring, "Don't be uptight, I said I'd do it, didn't I?" Or the anger hidden in the tardy dawdling can now be blamed openly on the other: "You're so impatient and critical, it's no wonder I use up the time I need to just work things out with you."

Procrastination is its own reward since it offers the impression that there are so many truly important things on the schedule that you don't have a chance to get all the trivial things done as well. *Important* includes all those things valued by you, *trivial* is the catchall for those things valued by the other person.

The inner dynamics of procrastination are similar to the interpersonal ones. The most typical procrastinator is divided within between an internal tyrant who demands that all things be done immediately, immaculately, with efficient dispatch and a resisting truant who resents being pushed. As always, the underdog truant triumphs. The passive fight style which works on the tyrant within also works on tyrants without.

The alternative to these passive games of slowly chipping away at other's abilities to cope, is to come to value the interactions of life as the real stuff of which friendship is made.

A friendship is as good as its faith in each others' trustworthiness is deep. A group is as healthy as its contract is clear. A marriage is as strong as its covenant is seen as sacred. And humans are as mature as their commitments to their colleagues are honored and celebrated.

Our personalities are composed of concentric ring on ring of promises made to ourselves and to others, of contracts struck and kept, of covenants pledged and honored. We may undercommit and live out the postponing, delaying, forgetful style of resistance to others. We may overcommit and slavishly comply with conventions, punctually live for deadlines and dates. We may miscommit to values that do not unite us with significant others in creative healthy community. Or we may fail on our commitments. The rings, tree-like, accumulate and the shape of a person's abilities to keep faith with self and others emerges as a person lives out the balance of freedom and responsibility, of duty and voluntary choice, of obligation and autonomy.

Wisdom emerges from experience as we are able to recognize (1) that life is promise, it is lived in the loving safety of promise freely made and gladly kept; (2) that identity is shaped most by our ability to keep faith with those we value; (3) that the meaningfulness of life is found in loving persons faithfully. Living well involves risking trusting and loving: risking promises that have depth and length; trusting the promises others make; and celebrating the love that keeps us both safely separate and securely connected to each other.

Dirty Fighting Code

"It was just an agreement, not a promise. I'll skip it and let them see how much they need me. It was a trivial thing, not important, I'll do it later and let them adjust. It wasn't important, forget it."

Fair Fighting Creed

"I will honor commitments, contracts, covenants as the building blocks of relationship. I will be open to your renegotiation, I will clearly recontract when I want change or release."

Exercises

1. On Procrastinating: Reflect on a job which you dislike and prefer to delay. Can you write out the inner dialogue which takes place between your inner tyrant and truant? If you cannot hear it, can you plan to listen carefully at the next instance of postponing to bring it up from the unconscious where it gets repressed?
2. On forgetting: Note the things forgotten in the recent past which caused disappointment in others. Can you identify the resistance or resentment in yourself which triggered the amnesia? How can you make notes in the future which will end this process and invite more direct expression of your frustration?

Day Twenty-Four

Mind Reading

Old Self Instructions

Mind read, mind rape

I have this hunch on what
you're meaning.
(I bet I'm right, why check
it out?)
I have this fantasy of
what you're thinking.
(I'm sure I'm right, why
ask your views?)
I have this suspicion of
what you're feeling.
(I'm no dummy, it's all
over your face.)
I have this conviction I
can read your mind.
(I know you better than
you know yourself.)

New Self Instructions

Listen, wait, learn

I will not
Hunch your thoughts,
Second-guess your
views,
Sense your wishes,
Suspect your motives,
Finish your sentences.
You alone can speak for
you.
You alone know your
heart.

"You don't mean that. I know you better than to believe that."
(what you really meant was . . .)

"What you were trying to say is . . . "
(let me speak for you, I can do it better)

"You're just jealous. I know it's hard for you to see me succeeding after all these years when you've been the one who was always on top."
(I can read your "jealousy" but am blind to mine)

"Love means you never have to ask for something that is really important to you. On such things, the other person knows what you need."

This myth about affectionate mind reading is similar to its more violent twin, the invasion of mind rape which penetrates the other's self-respect, dictates the other's thoughts, manipulates communication to coerce the other into thinking, feeling, acting as the manipulator wishes.

These are strong words used in description of such a common and seemingly innocuous pattern of coaching another in communication by second-guessing what is not said, reading between the lines of what is said, and trusting one's premonitions on what will be said.

Mind reading has a variety of levels.

Level One: Assuming understanding. The simplest and most casual form of mind reading occurs when one person assumes, without checking it out with the other, that a certain thought, feeling, emotion, attitude, or perception is being experienced. All listening is assuming followed by verifying; the listener assumes that the words heard, the tone and inflection received, the feelings and emotions expressed are combining to communicate the meaning interpreted in the hearer's mind. At best, the listener has only an inkling of what the other is experiencing.

Assumptions must be checked out against the following communications or clarified with a request for repetition or further explanation. Dirty fighting occurs when the hearer says: "I don't care what you say now, I heard you loud and clear and I know what you meant."

Level Two: Presuming knowledge. The second and more virulent form of mind reading occurs as one seeks to persuade another that "I know better than you what you are thinking, feeling, wanting, or needing."

I have every right to disagree with the accuracy of your thoughts or the appropriateness of certain wants. But you alone can speak for your feelings, express your thoughts, affirm your needs. My perceptions of what you are feeling or thinking will often be different from yours. I do trust my perceptions, they are my measures of reality, but when I insist that they are final for you as well as for me, I am acting in crazy-making ways. The best I can offer is a frank report on how I see you and be open to hear your confirmation or negation.[8]

Level Three: Ascribing motives. When the reader not only presumes knowledge but begins to impugn motives, someone is playing god. The function of labeling motives is to put down the other's intentions as unworthy or unacceptable. Invading another's head and judging his or her heart is a violation of the other's human dignity.

"You don't really mean that, you're just saying it because you're worn out." "You can't possibly mean that, you're just angry and trying to hurt me because you're jealous."

Such impugning of motives is unethical, unfair, as well as an impossible venture.

Level Four: Usurping control. In highly fused families, one member can claim the right to tell another what he or she can, may, does or doesn't think. This usurping of the other's personhood happens when parents tell children, "No, you don't want that, you want this." Or, "I know you didn't mean that, you wouldn't say that about your mother." Spouses usurp authority by claiming, "I know you say you're not going to the party, but I know you really want to be there."

Effective listening honors equal integrity between the hearer and speaker. Any impulse to sense another's wishes, guess another's wants or know another's motives must be canceled if either person's integrity is to be preserved. And an open interest in hearing the other share the personal wishes, wants, hopes, and thoughts from the privacy of his or her mind allows us to communicate with honesty and with the excitement of daily surprise.

Dirty Fighting Code

"I can nudge you with my hunches, direct you with my foresight, protect you with my insight since I know what is best for you and want only what is for your good."

Fair Fighting Creed

"I will not seek to limit your right or inhibit your freedom to speak frankly and choose freely what you see, think, feel, or want."

Exercises

To enrich listening skills, consider the following . . .

True	False	
____	____	1. I often speak more than my half in a conversation without giving the other equal time.
____	____	2. I sometimes share my thoughts and feelings without pausing to ask or wait for the view from the other side.
____	____	3. I don't mind when someone who knows me well finishes my sentences or speaks for me.
____	____	4. I often feel I know another well enough to be able to answer for most any issue that rises.
____	____	5. I can often read another by his or her facial signs or bodily signals as well as by his or her words.
____	____	6. I sometimes trust my picture of what is going on inside another much better than the description I get in the other's words.

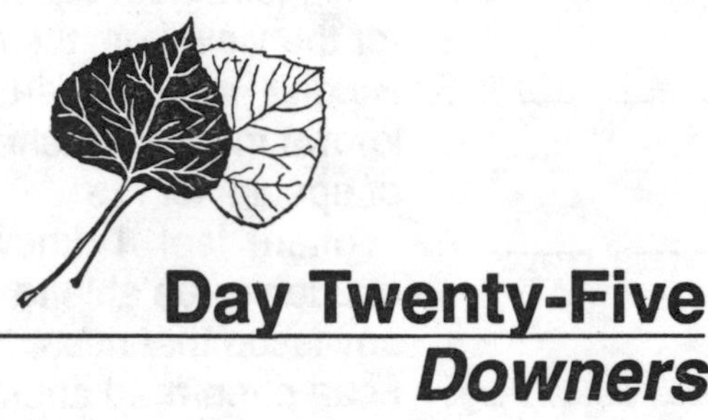

Day Twenty-Five
Downers

Old Self Instructions

Downers and put-downs

Practice the gentle art of
Dropping downers—
pry to push them off balance,
nag to raise irritation,
lecture to belittle,
nail them to trigger insecurity,
pigeonhole to cut down,
label to shut out.
Be subtle, be slick, be smooth.

New Self Instructions

Uppers and levelers

I am I,
I will be
Equal
(Even when devalued),
Level
(Even when belittled),
Caring
(Even when insulted),
Candid
(Even when avoided),
Authentic
(in all of the above).

"Why are you so clumsy? You've either three left hands or you're out to lunch!"
(father to son—translation: "You're a loser")

"You don't care if these children live or die. They'd get better care in an orphanage."
(wife to husband—translation: "You're a lousy father")

"When are you going to listen to me? You're always messing things up."
(employer to employee—translation: "Once more and you're out")

The world is full of downers, downers which can deflate the successful, humble the confident, reduce the proud. But their uses are far beyond these. Forceful downers can be used to correct, to discipline, to control, to manage, to direct. Subtle downers can be employed to belittle, to undermine, to probe, to nudge in desired directions.

To push others off balance, to trigger insecurity, to nag with constant irritation, to needle another to do whatever is wished without open confrontation, the downer is the perfect answer. Why confront when you can outwit?

"Downers" are any communication style or strategy which turns a horizontal relationship suddenly vertical. Downers can instantly convert a level or equal relationship into an unequal one by talking down, putting down, looking down on the other.

Returning a downer for a downer only increases the inequality and imbalance. The better alternative is to remain level no matter what the other offers, to give yourself the needed upper to counteract the downer even when the impact of the other's behavior is painful.[9]

To the nagging downer who asks, "When are you going to get started on this project?" give a level response which does not fudge, "I've not begun, when did you want it completed?" stays unhooked by the irritant in the question.

To the prying downer who says, "I know it's none of my business, and I probably shouldn't ask, but what are your . . . ?" make a simple response of, "If I don't want to answer, I'll let you know," reassures both of you that you won't get into an uncomfortable position in the name of politeness.

To the trapping downer who asks, "Do you have anything scheduled for next Sunday?" offer a simple, "Tell me what you have in mind" gets you off the spot.

To the eager advisor who volunteers, "If I were you I'd certainly try to . . . " a clear recognition of your own responsibility can be said with, "So that's what you would do . . . hmm . . . I'm still deciding my choice."

To the insulting downer who exclaims, "That's a mighty stupid thing to do!" a nondefensive response could be, "What looks stupid to one person sometimes turns out to be pretty wise for another."

To the analyst who pronounces, "You couldn't handle that job, you're much too quiet and shy," a self-affirmation is useful, "Yes, I do have a quiet, shy side, I also have a very confident side that you may not have seen."

To the lecturing downer who delivers a sermonette: "We should all learn to be more understanding and cooperative around here so that there would be less conflict," one asks for concrete suggestions, "What changes would you suggest for reducing tension?"

All of these, given in a nondefensive tone of voice,

remain level, equal, and horizontal. The tension is reduced when one does not give downer for downer, dig for dig.

Recognizing that any criticism offered is a critique of a part, not the whole, sets the recipient free to accept it as that person's commentary on that one facet of the person or personality. Even when the criticism is given in general, inclusive, or total language, the receiver can accept it, making clear it is only a part of the self being criticized and affirming that there is much more.

The goal of staying on even ground is not easily reached. Rehearsal of appropriate responses to others' habitual downers can help one prepare new statements and add them to the behavioral repertoire. Each time one is hooked by a downer and nudged into inferior or depressive feelings, can become an example for reflection and creation of a new response for use when the situation returns. Being such creatures of habit, human beings can be counted on to give you the opportunity to test any planned response. Reflect. Review. Rehearse. Recreate!

Dirty Fighting Code

Sneak in a downer, slip in a criticism, drop in a dig, toss in a comment; all of these serve to bring the other down.

Fair Fighting Creed

Stay level—we are in two-way conversation with each other; stay equal—we are in two-way negotiation with each other; stay real—we can get on with two-way friendship even through ups and downs.

Exercises

1. Review your list of six most difficult downers.

Write out nondefensive, level responses which fit you. Practice them with an imaginary person in an empty chair.

2. Reread the examples in this chapter. Note how many of these downer statements or questions may be unintentional slights which express old habitual ways of communication. How can you stay unhooked, unirritated, and undestroyed by these?

Day Twenty-Six

Suspecting

Old Self Instructions

Be jealous, be possessive

You are untrustworthy,
You have to be watched.
You are causing me pain.
(I would not be
suspicious,
Mistrustful, or jealous
If it weren't for you
And your wandering eye,
Your contagious smile,
Your constant warmth.)
So you must change,
Withdraw as I prescribe,
Avoid all temptation,
Before I can trust you.

New Self Instructions

Love sets free

I want to trust you,
I some times feel jealous.
I want to believe you.
I some days feel anxious.
I want to respect you,
I some moments suspect
you.
I will own my anxiety,
My suspicion, my
mistrust.
They are my fears, my
demands.
I cancel them in love.

"You are working with so many interesting and attractive men at the office, I sometimes feel such deep pangs of jealousy. I'm not blaming you for them. I just want you to know what I fight inside."
(clean, clear ownership of feelings)

"I saw the way you looked at her, it just cut through me like a knife. I don't trust her and I don't want you working close to her again."
(mixed, blaming, mistrusting and controlling feelings)

"Once I found out about his record I just couldn't feel the same working with him again. Once a man's hand is in the till, you don't tempt him again."
(pure suspicion, with no present evidence)

There's an illusion of power in suspicion. The suspecting one seizes on some bit of history, some curious behavior, some threatening circumstance. Some compromising possibility creates a theory, and acts as though it were true. The power springs from the illusions of foreknowledge (I just knew it would happen), and foresight (I've seen it coming for some time but I didn't want to believe it), coupled with foreboding (I would think you would be grateful, I'm only watching out for your welfare) and the threat of the forecast (If it breaks wide open, I don't know what I'll do). The function of such suspicion is to keep not only the self but also the other in suspense.

Suspicion and jealousy are twin emotions. The word *suspicion* is used to designate the more negative, hostile, and fearful pole which precedes exposure and rejection of a betrayer or an enemy, and jealousy to describe the warmer emotion of threatened love, anxious affection, and possessive manipulation. However both emotions can mix hot and cold, love and hate, acceptance and rejection.

Of course, both of these emotions are normal and appropriate when there is actual, objective provocation by the other person in a relationship. In marriage, the desire for sexual exclusiveness, the commitment to fidelity, the need for emotional priority in the mate's life, the assurance that the primary commitment is safe, all of these are fundamental motivations for the security of the loving relationship. A partner who gets jealous in response to actual provocative threats on any of these is not necessarily a jealous spouse. But if the response is out of proportion to the provocation or if he begins to look for occasions to be jealous, or if when none appear she imagines them, or if incidental things get exaggerated interpretations in his mind, then the jealousy is becoming obsessive and turning into hostile suspicion.

It is important to differentiate between natural and obsessive jealousy, because all jealous persons explain their feelings in the name of love, but the love shown is a possessive, absorbing concern that leads to strangulation. Although love has its own fears about loss and its own drives to possess, at the core of the emotion is a deep concern for the other's freedom. The more I love you, the more I set you free, so any relationship which feels more like suffocation is something more than love.

Love reclaims the responsibility for its own fears, anxieties, and obsessions and restores the freedom between lover and loved.

When one doubts another and the other protests innocence, there is no way out of the cyclical dance. As long as the onus is on the accused party to prove trustworthiness, both lose. If I question your trustworthiness a condition of inequality is created as I become both prosecutor and judge. If you seek to prove yourself, the vertical distance is increased. If you refuse, the resulting distance remains.

If instead, the one who does not feel trusting can recognize the loss of the ability to be trusting is a problem to be owned, shared, and worked out without accusations or put-downs, then the two can explore what is alienating the one from the other, or both from each other.

It may be a momentary loss of self-esteem which is triggering the suspicion impulse and inviting the person to compare the self with others. Sharing it may help restore the self-valuing.

It may be conditioning from childhood to have difficulty trusting anyone in times of stress (or particularly men, women, authority figures, professionals, etc.). If I can own my tendency to mistrust, I can grow.

It may be that I have learned to expect virtual perfection from others, assuming that they will make no mistakes, and to mistrust them forever if they make even one mistake.

It may be that I am picking up some other signal from you—your frustration, loneliness, exhaustion, burnout—and misreading it according to my fears.

Or it may be true that there is a reason for my mistrust that you will be able to voluntarily share and resolve with me.

Whatever option occurs of these or the many more possibilities, the best route is for the anxious party to own, express, and deal with the anxiety without laying the cause immediately at the other's doorstep. When such honesty and self-responsibility is practiced, we have a much better chance at either regaining trust or finding out that trust is no longer appropriate. Either option is preferable to the long-term ulceration of chronic unresolved suspicion. Either is a step toward the freedom that nourishes love.

Dirty Fighting Code

"When I am jealous, it is your duplicity we must examine. When I am suspicious, it is your fidelity we must test. When I have doubts, you are on trial."

Fair Fighting Creed

"When I am anxious, fearful, mistrusting, jealous, or suspicious, the feelings are mine. I will work through them to deal with my fears. If I discover that the occasion lies between us, or you own it as yours, we can then take appropriate steps toward resolution."

Exercises

1. Finish the lines: "When I feel jealous, I fear the loss of . . ."; "I want to take control of . . ."
2. Explain the various reasons given above for the rise of jealous or suspicious feelings. Which have you experienced?
3. For discussion with a partner: "Which route do we take when one of us is suspicious—locating the problem in the other or owning it as pain within the self?"

Day Twenty-Seven
Projecting

Old Self Instructions

"You" message expose you

You are the problem in any conflict.
You must be described, analyzed, diagnosed.
You must be confronted, lectured, persuaded.
You must be threatened, warned, punished.
You must be directed, ordered, commanded.
You must be criticized, labeled.
You must be exposed.

New Self Instructions

"I" messages reveal me

I can only speak to my part of the problem.
I can only express my thoughts and feelings.
I can best reach you by self-disclosing.
I can gain more from you by actively listening.
I can find out your thoughts by inviting you to share them.
I can move toward you by opening myself.
I will share myself.

"You're angry at me, that's what; but you just won't admit that's what's behind that sweet smile!"
(I am reading your mind; unfair)

"You're just uptight because you felt abandoned in childhood and you can't stand being rejected now."
(I'm telling your story; unkind)

"You've been avoiding me all day long, there's obviously something bothering you. Why don't you come out with it?"
(I'm doing your work, I think; actually I'm sticking you with my problems)

When in conflict, "you-messages" put the ball in the other's court; "you-language" puts the blame on the other person; "you-statements" keep the focus off of you and your problems and on the other. "You-sentences" project one's own pain onto the other person.

(Never mind that you-messages are self-defeating since no one can speak for another; self-destructive since the more one seeks to read another's mind, the less one knows one's own; and self-serving since defining any conflict as primarily the other person's insensitivity, rigidity, or stupidity is a self-protective dodge.)

When in conflict, the shortest route to new healing understanding is by way of I-messages. They offer honesty, accuracy, and deeper levels of intimacy by self-disclosing what is truly seen, felt, thought by at least one person in the dialogue.

An I-message offers many advantages over any other form of self-expression in times of stress.

"You are a liar" makes a judgment which cuts off

communication. "I don't believe you" is an I-message which reports my puzzlement.

"You're not listening" is an evaluation which rarely improves the other's listening skills. "I don't feel heard" reports my loneliness.

"You better cut it out this minute or . . . " is a command threat which produces resentment, resistance, and often rebellion. "I'm tired of the way things have been going, I want to work out something different," uses the power of self-disclosing.

"You're just hostile to men and I happen to be the available one" is an analysis which threatens the other's privacy. "I'm willing to hear your anger, I need some help knowing how much of it really belongs to me" reveals my confusion mixed with caring.

"You must have done something to cause it; are you telling the whole truth?" is a cross-examination which alienates. "I need to know more about what happened, tell me more" uses the power of invitation.

The purpose of communication is to arrive at common understandings, and when the issues focus on inviting change in a relationship, it makes the most sense to send the message in a way that creates as little defensiveness as is possible. The you-message is full of burrs and thorns. It creates barriers rather than removing them, destroys the mutual respect needed to resolve tension rather than creating it.

I-messages are confessional, self-revealing, invitational, and expressive of one's own unique experience without attacking, belittling, or downplaying the other's own perspective.

The I-message is the most direct way of describing the speaker's perceptions and feelings, but without the implication that the other was the cause of those feelings. It offers the frank admission of one's own perspectives without projecting them on to the other person.

Although I-messages may reduce defensiveness, they do not eliminate it. Any clear statement which calls another to see things in an alternate way will evoke defensive feelings and words. But how much better to deal with defenses to the real message intended rather than to the secondary irritation caused by the offensive style.

The goal of clear communication is to increase the amount of available information between persons so that more free, more just, more mutually satisfactory solutions may be found. Confessional statements add to the shared data; judgmental comments about the other subtract.

When in stress, it is wise to avoid questions, discard you-messages and speak for yourself, from yourself, of your own values and views.

Dirty Fighting Code

"You can't solve our problem, you are the problem, you must change as I prescribe."

Fair Fighting Creed

"I will share my perceptions, speak my emotions, affirm my intentions in simple, direct speech."

Exercises

1. Reflect on the most recent conflict. Recall the three things you most wanted to communicate. Express these in you-messages. Note all the ways these can be misunderstood or misperceived. Now phrase them in I-messages. Evaluate their strengths and weaknesses.
2. For one day, speak only in I-statements. Note their ease, impact, clarity.

Day Twenty-Eight
Disarming

Old Self Instructions

Going for the kill

If possible,
Intimidate.
If necessary,
Annihilate.
But never
hesitate,
Or you lose.
(There are no beltlines,
no safety zones,
In the end,
you're alone!)

New Self Instructions

Honoring the belt line

Never use
the final weapon,
Never play
the last card,
Never attack
the bottom line
Or you both lose.
(What is the profit
If you win the whole
world
And lose your integrity?
You're alone!)

"I didn't want to say this, but you've driven me to it, you are just like . . . "
(everyone has a vulnerable spot; to win, strike beneath the belt)

"How dare you criticize me for that when we both know how you . . . "
(everyone has a painful memory; to win, bring it out to disarm them)

"Do I need to remind you of . . . "
(Everyone has a secret; to know it is to overpower them)

Everyone has a weak point, a painful secret, a vulnerable spot which is guarded lest it be used to do them in. It may vary from an embarrassing incident to a devastating instance of shame. Or it may be a frustrating handicap or a traumatic experience of childhood. It may be a personal failure or a family scandal or skeleton in the closet.

The skilled dirty fighter can sense these things, and when the other must be totally disarmed he goes for the jugular.

The urge to incapacitate the opponent in conflict rises as desperation overwhelms human concern for the other's welfare, and winning becomes everything.

The willingness to use anything, when "going for the kill," may rise not only out of a need to win at any cost, it may be motivated by the terrible fears of being destroyed or found out. Many people harbor such terror which can make almost any difference look like a survival issue where all is at stake, so all must be thrown into the battle. The three most common annihilation tactics are called hitting below the belt, striking the Achilles' heel, going for the throat. Not nice names for a very nasty motive.[10]

Each person has a belt line, whether stated and thus fully recognized by the other, or unstated and therefore sensed by the sudden rise of anxiety or the feeling of being fouled. The belt line marks the individual's "safe zones" that can be challenged or critiqued in a hassle. Blows scored beneath that line are felt to be intolerable. Where friends, partners, family know that line, such a blow is a violation of trust.

One person's line may be drawn at swearing or obscene language, another feels devastated by yelling or temper outbursts, while others find silent withdrawal and cold hostile coexistence are impossible to face.

An Achilles' heel is an area of weakness in which an attack feels so overwhelmingly destructive that one is rendered painfully vulnerable. A psychological concern—such as a tendency toward depression, a social fear—such as the memory of a humiliating failure, an economic failure—such as a lamented misjudgment, a physical handicap—an unchangeable disability, one or all of these areas may hide a tender spot which has been revealed in intimacy. To strike the blow in such an area cuts to the quick of a relationship.

Going for the throat needs no further explanation. It is an overkill strategy which uses such measures of insult and injury that the whole basis of mutuality and cooperation is destroyed and must be rebuilt from scratch if it is to exist again.

The impulse to disarm the other must be itself disarmed. Fair fighting respects the primary commitments of good will that guard each other's safety and security. The boundary lines of privacy, the belt lines of vulnerability, the Achilles' heels of disability are all laid aside as inappropriate targets. Under no circumstances are they fair tools in the give and take of even the most heated debate.

All effective conflict is over secondary issues of difference. The primary issues of our fellow-feeling for the other must be accepted as the floor on which all negotiation and management of frustration stands. We share our co-humanity. We are sisters and brothers. We will stand with each other, come what will or what may.

Dirty Fighting Code

There's always the last resort, and the real fighter knows what to use, how to use it, and when to spring the surprise.

Fair Fighting Creed

To know another's weakness and to never use it, to share another's confidence and never abuse it, to see another's vulnerability and respect it is to join with humanity.

Exercises

1. Locate your belt line. List those issues that are beneath it. Is it too high? Can you lower it and still be safe? Can you discuss it with one important person in your life?
2. Reflect on those vulnerable spots in your spouse, your children, your associates that you have been tempted to use. Pledge your respect.

Day Twenty-Nine
Guarding

Old Self Instructions

Demand guarantees

Insist on unconditional vows.
Demand absolute pledges.
Exact unlimited loyalties.
Require ironclad guarantees.
All or nothing.
Forever.

New Self Instructions

Forego, forgive, forget

Forego demands on the future,
We cannot control the uncontrollable.
Forget demands on the past,
We cannot change the unchangeable.
Forgive the demands of the present,
We can work through differences now.

"How can I be sure that this will never happen again? I need some evidence, some guarantee."
(there are no ironclad guarantees among the living, only among the dead)

"So you say you're sorry, you look sorry and you act sorry, but you're not sorry, not as sorry as you will be!"
(there are no punishments, no penalties or penance that can control the future)

"I guess we do deserve each other, you can forgive but you can't forget, I can forget but I can't forgive."
(forgiveness opens the future once more and sets both the forgiver and the forgiven free)

"How am I supposed to trust you further after you've gone back on your word so often?" The wish to freeze the future so that it is no longer uncertain is most intense in those who want ironclad guarantees that an injury, insult or injustice will never be repeated.

But the future cannot be determined by either the angry person demanding unconditional promises of the desired perfection nor by the guilty person seeking to reassure the other that intentions are genuine. In fact, genuine intentions of renewed fidelity or consistency are all we have to offer one another. The demand for more is a strategy which allows us to exact penance or extract some penalty from the other. It is a sign that the anger is still not fully resolved and the reconciliation is premature.

The future is beyond our control. The fantasy that one's anger is sufficiently powerful to control the uncontrollable is a godlike pretention which must be cancelled in simply coming to terms with reality. What has happened, *was*. What we are now pledging as intentions, *is*. What will be, *will be*. The impulses of the future and their direction are dependent not on the intensity of our control strategies but on our integrity in giving up control and accepting the uncertainties of commitment. Maturity is the willingness to forego demands on the future.

The past is outside our grasp. What has taken place now exists in our memories and will not be changed by our working through. The meaning will be altered and integrated into our new understandings of each other, but the actual event cannot be erased. The fantasy that one can change the unchangeable by dent of one's resentment must be cancelled. Maturity is to accept the reality of what has occurred, and to actively change its impact now.

The present is ours. If we are to rebuild what lies between us we must accept the task of renegotiating our faith in each other, repenting of the ways that faith has been betrayed, and recommitting ourselves to keep faith in days to come.

Forgiveness is the mutual recognition that repentance is perceived as genuine and right relationships have now been achieved. The task of working out this mutual resolution requires that we deal with our anger toward the past—resentment—but without holding on to the past with a bulldog bite. It requires letting go. Then the second task is confronting our suspicions toward the future without holding back in frozen fear. It requires letting be what will be.

Now forgetting can do its important work.

Forgiving and forgetting are related to each other, but forgiving always precedes forgetting. To forgive, one must remember the injury, the impact, the injustice done. Before one can fully forgive and forget, both the offender and the offended must recall the wrongdoing together, release the feelings together, remember the pain together, reconstruct the relationship together, and then they may forget together.[11]

Forgetting without first forgiving is a negation of what actually happened and of the integrity and reality of memory. Forgiving is a positive process that recognizes the needs of both the offender and the offended, brings these into the open, and resolves them in the creation of new relationship without ironclad guarantees, but with something better, living growing intentions.

Dirty Fighting Code

"Fooled me once, shame on you; twice, shame on me. I never forget an injury, never forgive an injustice without absolute proof of change. Since that takes a lifetime of observation to prove such a guarantee, I'm willing to wait and watch."

Fair Fighting Creed

"I will face the past with you, recall, rework, and reconstruct its residues. I will meet you in the present on the basis of our mutual genuineness. I will join you in entering an open future."

Exercises

1. To release the past, affirm for yourself: "I am not my past. I am enriched or impoverished by its choices. I am responsible for their resolution here and now." Do you agree? Can you identify the freedoms which this affirmation offers? Can you affirm it of those you love? Of those you dislike? Of an enemy you resent?
2. To reach out to the future, confess of yourself. "I have no power to control, shape, direct, deter-

mine the future. I can choose what I value, pledge what I intend, commit myself to what I hold sacred." Do you ask more of yourself? Do you demand more of others?

Day Thirty
Perfection

Old Self Instructions

Fight perfectly

Fight fairly.
Fight flawlessly.
Fight faultlessly.
The minimum
requirement is
Perfection.

New Self Instructions

Fight creatively

I change . . .
Not when I am trying
to be what I am not,
But when I fully accept
What I truly am.

"If it weren't for you, ours would have been a perfect marriage."
(except for an obvious lack of humility in one partner)

"I would think you would consider it a privilege to be married to someone who fights as clean as I."
(you just blew it in the last line)

"If we could just agree to follow the rules of fair fighting it would remove a lot of the tension between us."
(choosing values and styles that are more fair can set both free, but imposing or obeying rules creates more new tensions than it resolves)

The temptation to become healthy by imitating healthy people is an immensely attractive shortcut for many people. It is a detour. Attempting to discipline, drive, or hypnotize oneself into feeling healthful feelings, experiencing only positive emotional responses, is a self-defeating change strategy. More healthful models of fighting fairly and feeling more positively can be learned, but they must arise from choices desired, wanted, claimed from within.

When a person attempts to suppress "bad" feelings or destructive impulses and force "good" emotions by driving toward constructive responses, an inner conflict is created which at best makes the attempt feel unnatural and uncomfortable, and at worst sabotages the whole process, creating depression and a sense of defeat.

Incorporating the fair fighting models into an ideal self which is demanding change, or into a strict conscience which adds them to its already bulging collection of moral restrictions, only tends to increase the internal binds and conflicts.

The path to increased health leads not toward perfection but toward completeness. Perfection is not a desirable outcome since it ultimately alienates persons and distances them from each other. Completeness fills out the missing parts of ourselves, finishes the unfinished tasks of our childhood and adolescent development, and makes more of our inner resources available for relationship.

The goal is not to eliminate but to limit the unfair behaviors or dirty fighting impulses. These continue to spring up from the inner creativity of the truly spontaneous person. The goal is to recognize them more quickly as they rise, and be able to refuse them and choose more fair, more effective responses. Where it once took six months to realize what was going wrong, growth means that it now becomes clear in six weeks, or six days, or six hours, or six minutes. When one can see what is going wrong in six seconds, real freedom is being felt.

Perfectionist demands self-destruct. As the pressure comes to conform to the rules, directions, or models which have been swallowed whole and applied in undigested form, an equal and opposite resistance is expressed by the underside of the personality. Both sides, ideal and real, must come together for real growth to occur.

Three continuing rules of human growth are:

One: I change, not when I am trying to be what I am not but when I am fully accepting what I am.

Two: I grow, not when I am trying to behave as I should or ought but when I am choosing what I truly want.

Three: I am becoming, not when I am trying to be perfect, or seeking to direct new behavior with pressure and demands but when I am cherishing fully who I am and choosing freely who I am becoming.

Not perfection, but completeness is the goal.
Not instant maturity, but intentional maturing is the goal.
Not utterly fair fighting, but new fairness in the fight.

Dirty Fighting Code

"I will fight right, without failing no matter what the other does. My model will show what we should be doing, ought to value, must achieve."

Fair Fighting Creed

"I will seek to be more available, more present, more complete, more aware of our equal preciousness in good moments and in bad."

Exercises

List five faults that you find in your fight style. Write them out in clear declarative sentences, such as:

"I hide my anger and later ventilate rage."

"I catch them by surprise with bad timing."

Now rewrite these sentences as demands from your ideal self. For example:

"My ideal self deals with anger simply, clearly, immediately, and has nothing reserved to ventilate later."

"My ideal self fights only by appointment, and seeks a time that is mutually acceptable to both."

Now compare these statements with your inner experience. Does your ideal self command, demand, nudge you toward change?

1. Relax this inner muscle that drives you.
2. Bring the two sides into conversation.
3. Make peace between the ideal and the real.
4. Now, what change do you really want?

Epilogue

Caring-Fighting—Creating Equal Relationships

"There are no equal relationships. One party is always more equal than the other."
(this objection rises from either oppressor or oppressed, but not from one who is experiencing equality)

"Someone has to have the last word. Sooner or later, when push comes to shove, there must be somebody in charge."
(this conviction assumes a deadlock; an alternative view is that any decision which must be decided unilaterally is better not made)

"Isn't it inappropriate to even raise the question of equal relationships among Christians? We are called

of God to find our place in submission to the order of headship."
(the question of equality was raised by Moses, Hosea, Micah, Jesus, John, Paul, among others)

The quality of your and my life is best measured by the quality of the relationships we are able to create with those about us.

One-up-and-one-down relationships of claimed superiority demean both the pretender to the throne and the one beneath. As relationships are ranked in vertical measures of worth, significance, or dignity, the dignity and humanity of all of us are lessened. The inevitable differences of privilege and responsibility, of tasks and accountability which emerge in all relationships can be assigned, recognized, and exercised without the elevation of one and the subordination of the other.

In equal relationships, there may be rich varieties of preferences, gifts, interests, and tasks assigned, but each has equal rights, equal responsibility for the decisions made, equal freedom to call for renegotiation.

Relationships vary greatly in the degree of equality provided by their agreements or understandings. There are three basic types of interpersonal relationships, based on how control is distributed between the two. The three are *Complementary*—where contrasting persons connect to each fulfill the other's missing parts; *Symmetrical*—where both strive to keep everything perfectly balanced; and *Parallel*—where each person claims the equality within the safety of mutual freedom and commitment. The first looks backward to continue what was—tradition—the second looks both inward and outward in both separate and opposite directions. The third looks forward together.[12]

Complementary Relationships

Complementary relationships fit together like hand and glove, day and night.

Complementary relationships are based on the belief that in any dyad one must define or lead and the other reply or follow. ("I'm in charge now!" "That's O.K. with me.") Or one must rescue and save while the other enjoys the dependency and attention. ("I need someone to help me." "Right, here I am.")

Contrast between the two and the constant maximization of differences are seen as the way to complete and fulfill the other. Coordination of activities is easier to attain and maintain once each has accepted an "up" or "down" position. Collaboration is simple since one leads, the other follows.

In conflict, the participants choose matching styles, for example, aggressive control and accommodating niceness, or authoritarian demands and complying kindness. So one demands, the other yields, or one seduces, the other submits.

In its most positive form, this allows partners to feel safe in predicting outcomes of any conflict or to form definite images of the other's response under stress. Since it is certain that one will wield power, and the other yield, the end is safely clear.

Its negative impact is deep. Both persons lose freedom to choose since one always submits, the other dominates. Change, development, and creative marital evolution throughout the life cycle are blocked and frequently become oppressive. Any change threatens the self-definition of both.

Symmetrical Relationships

Symmetrical relationships are like a tug-of-war, a seesaw.

Complementary Relationships	*Symmetrical Relationships*	*Parallel Relationships*
I am I (You are what I'm not). I am I (You are my shadow). I am I (You are my better half).	I am Me BUT You want to be You. I can't be my way Because You are being your way. I insist on my dream BUT You insist on your dream.	I am I AND You are you. As I am solely I, AND you are fully you, We are truly we. I will be all that I can be. Come, be all you can be.

Symmetrical relationships are based on the belief that both persons have an equal right to define their relationship in all areas. "I have just as much right to define us as you do, I'm just as good as you are. You can't tell me what to do!" "Right-wrong," "'tis-'taint."

Absolute equality and the minimization of difference are constantly stressed as both seek to assert the same type of control in all areas. This creates a fragile and tension-filled or a coldly mathematical relationship in working out perfect fairness in the status struggle.

In its positive mode, two partners or co-workers with collaborative styles can work for mutual, equal, balanced resolutions in a symmetrical system. Frequently they will understand each other very well since similar stance and goals are practiced and desired.

In its more frequent negative mode, striving for the same turf and using the same style of conflict produces an unhealthy competition, a state of constant one-upmanship. Little gets invested in understanding the other's evaluation of him or her, much time is put into rejecting the other's point of view and proving the superiority or the equal dignity of one's own.

Parallel Relationships

Parallel relationships are like two walking hand-in-hand.

Parallel relationships are based on the belief that recognition, appreciation, and expression of differences can occur in give-and-take. "I am I, you are you, we together work out how we can be. Your freedom and fulfillment is as important as my own."

Fulfillment, development, and creative change are occurring in a context of trust, mutual respect, and tolerance of differences. Each has separate areas of con-

Three Styles of Marriage

Complementary Marriage	*Symmetrical Marriage*	*Parallel Marriage*
Each knows own role, place, task, responsibilities.	Both seek balanced roles with equal tasks, equal rights, privileges.	Both share, exchange, delegate, assign and reassign functions.
Identities of each are dependent.	Identities of both are counter-dependent as each asserts and defends independence.	Identity of each as separate, individuated, centered in personhood.
Identity is defined by the role, parent, partner, profession, performance.	Identity is connected to role, career, performance, success.	Identity is in being a person, disconnected from role, career, performance.
Each is what the other is not in reactive balancing.		

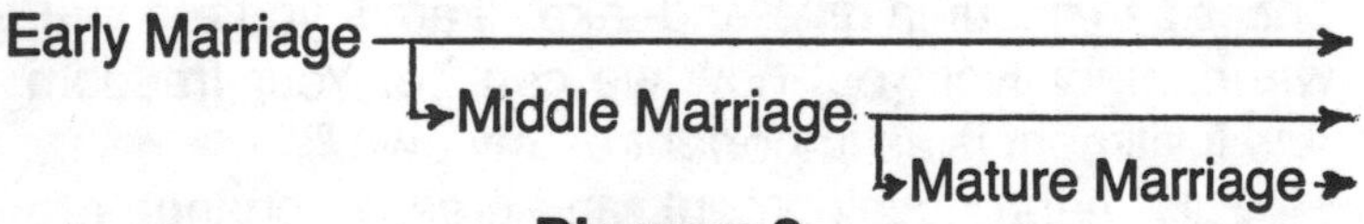

Early Marriage →
→ Middle Marriage →
→ Mature Marriage →

Diagram 2

trol to which the other defers, both share control in joint issues. Their styles are less rigid, patterned, or reactive to each other. Thus they can freely vary between complementary, symmetrical, and shared styles of resolving a conflict when the situation is appropriate. Some conflicts can be resolved in complementary recognition of another's strength in areas of one's own weakness. Others deserve a symmetrical hassle in pressing for equal symmetrical justice. And some are resolved immediately in shared yet parallel paths which respect both persons' needs and capabilities; so both win, both increase in power, both become more in control without subtracting from the other.

In its positive mode this allows each to develop a separate portion of the joint goals even by contrasting pathways, resources, and means, yet with shared results.

In its negative mode, the two may become divergent lines, not parallel, gradually growing apart unless clear covenants, shared time, and mutual benefits are renewed and reaffirmed.

Conflict in Three Relationships

The three basic types of relationship have three consequent conflict styles: suppression, competition, and cooperation. Three central rules emerge from observation, research, and therapy of all three.

One, *in the complementary marriage, effective negotiation and creatively mutual solutions are impossible.* As sociologist John Scanzoni concludes, "Persons who accept a hierarchical view of marriage will never be able to negotiate effectively or engage in creative conflict with their spouses."[13] Historically, the word *negotiate* was not in a king's vocabulary, his was the right to rule, and decree. The pope did not need to par-

Conflict in Complementary Marriage	***Conflict in Symmetrical Marriage***	***Conflict in Parallel Marriage***
Conflict is Suppressed	*Conflict is Cyclical*	*Conflict is Negotiated*
The paired problems of dominance and submission, aggression and accommodation, seduction and attraction, blaming and placating, computing and distracting lead to one-way solutions, one-up victories. One person wins, the other loses.	The balancing act or tug of war between two symmetrically paired persons with a fixed rigid and demanding view of equality creates cyclical conflict with persons alternating in dominance and submission, blaming and placating, and other paired wrestling matches where both lose.	The parallel presence of two centered persons allows them to deal with the contrast of differences and the clash of similarities in equal negotiation for equal satisfaction so that both win.
We Complement	*We Compete*	*We Cooperate*

ley. His was the privilege of pontification. And in hierarchical relationships, the one above retains the final word. Someone expresses, the other suppresses. One decides, the other defers.

Although in intimate loving relationships the atmosphere of concern for the other may create a benevolent authority pattern which ultimately serves the interests and the welfare of both in as far as they are aware, the one is still assumed into the other's presumption, and in stress the one is absorbed into the other's dominance.

Two, *in symmetrical marriage, effective negotiation is blocked by the reactive defensiveness of both.* The cyclical strategies of dividing all privilege and responsibility with exactness and measured fairness, and the competitive tension which heightens negative feelings make effective conflict highly unlikely.

Getting hooked emotionally in any conflict tends to trigger the mirror reaction of giving back what one is getting, or the mote-beam response of seeing the fault in the other that is invisible in the self, or the double-standard solution of excusing in one's own behavior the very thing one is accusing in the other. These cyclical dances tend to turn into negative spirals of decreasing freedom and increasing velocity and intensity.

Three, *in parallel marriages, the equidistance of the two pathways are maintained indefinitely by the connections made by covenants and the corrections forged through conflicts.* The two crucial forces of all human relationships—the attraction toward union and the affirmation of separation—are kept in creative tension by the agreements we work out and the conflicts we work through. The agreements are primary, the conflicts secondary. A basic structure of understandings, which we call *covenant,* unites the two in parallel tracks of friendship and companionship. Then secondary differences that both complicate and excite life can be negotiated.

Effective Marriage

An effective marriage must have a set of basic commitments which provide a floor of security and upon which conflict over the secondary issues may be waged creatively.

Effective marriage is based on the traditional values—fidelity and stability and on two nontraditional values—mutuality and equality.

Two major types of conflict occur within marriage. The first is a negative or basic conflict which could terminate the entire relationship because the foundational values and goals are being reviewed or revised. The second is a positive secondary conflict which challenges the many second-level understandings and agreements but the tensions are safe because the primary values are firm beneath them.

In the previous generations, the three basic values of marriage were hierarchy, fidelity, and stability (or permanence). When one or more of these was challenged, the marriage faltered. Today an increased concern for justice in relationships has altered these primal marital values. Mutuality and equality have replaced hierarchy.

In the shifting values of the mid-twentieth century many couples took mutuality and equality as the only basic nonnegotiable commitments, and viewed fidelity and stability as secondary in importance, negotiable, and/or optional. The research findings on the human experience that resulted have shown a renewed recognition that all four of these are basic, nonnegotiable values, and the violation of either or both disrupts the marriage and delays or damages personal growth. All four are crucial, foundational, integral to a just and lasting relationship.

When equality and mutuality replace hierarchy in the basic values, then neither person feels he or she has ultimate power over the other. Such power was illusory anyway, since an essential characteristic of humanness is to possess the power of rational, responsible self-direction. The only power truly human people seek is control over the self which invites others to take control of their lives. The old ways of domination of one sex over the other were not working in a context where justice had become a concern of open discussion. As long as concern for justice was only expressed to fellow*men*, hierarchy, domination, and submission could continue even in the intimacy of love relationships. No more can such suppression of the natural moral awareness succeed. Justice calls for equal regard with all associates and intimates, women and men.

The Equal Marriage

Equality in marriage is the fulfillment of the biblical teachings of justice, righteousness, and love.

Justice is equal concern for each person's full experience of life.

Justice, throughout the prophets and in the Gospels and Epistles, is a call for redemptive redistribution of resources, opportunity, and power and for the recognition of full personal responsibility and voluntary choice.

Righteousness is right relationships.

Righteousness in both the Old and New Testaments is viewed not as perfection but as right relation-

Positive Conflict	***Negative Conflict***
Secondary Values	Secondary Values
Primary Values 1 2 3 4	Primary Values
In positive, functional conflicts, the primary values hold firm as a floor of commitment; the secondary issues can then be resolved, strengthening the relationship	In negative, dysfunctional conflicts, the tensions in secondary values break through the floor of commitment and rupture the primary values, severing the relationship.

Diagram 3

ships—relationships which live out justice. The connection between these two is so tight that, in both Hebrew and Greek, the concepts must be translated in hyphenated twin-ship. Justice-righteousness is the central concern of Jesus' ethics and of Paul's teaching on integrity in life just as it was for Isaiah, Amos, Hosea, Micah, Jeremiah.

Love is equal regard.

Love in both testaments is most fully expressed in equal regard. The love which values self and other, self and neighbor, self and marital partner equally is seen as the heart of caring relationships. Such equal regard may be self-sacrificial, altruistic, benevolent, but the foundational element is the equal regard which prizes the other as the self.

Two arguments are frequently offered against the recognition of equality as the direction and intention of biblical teaching.

One. There are specific biblical texts which offer hierarchical teaching on male-female and husband-wife relationships.

Two. There is only one model for male-female, husband-wife relationships and the hierarchical model must be a central element in all teaching.

The situation is not so simple as this assumes. There is more than one model for these relationships in the New Testament. In fact, multiple models are offered in the Apostle Paul's writings and he shows no need to harmonize or to force them into one model for all persons. The hierarchical model of 1 Corinthians 11 includes a model of interdependency within the same passage. The Ephesians 5 model calls for a redefinition of the old hierarchical model to a new mutual submission marriage which works toward equality by demanding radical sacrifice on the part of the males to revolutionize the status quo. Paul's references to Peter's dominance and his wife's submission, Luke's account of Priscilla's outstanding leadership along with Aquilla's (Acts 18:26; Romans 16:3) and over a dozen other examples of joint ministry, full recognition of women in ministry, honoring the gifts of women in prophesy, leadership, teaching, and service indicates the trajectory of the new community in which—in Christ—there is neither male nor female. Just as there are no longer ethnic hierarchies nor slave and master hierarchies, so sexual hierarchies have come to an end (Gal. 3:28).

In the midst of the rich variety of models for marriages and relationships which the Bible offers in its marvelously accurate portrayals of humans at both their best and worst, there is a progression, a movement, a trajectory of the teaching which moves from women as possessions, to persons, to full equals. Parallel trajectories in other areas of human relations move from corporate-tribal views of personality, in which the whole family is destroyed for the sin of one member, to the full recognition of individual responsibility; from feudal monarchy to communal solidarity, from owner-slave economies to free and equal human community; from subordinated members under powerful priests and holy men to brother-sisterhood churches of equal members; from parents as possessing life-and-death power over children who owe them absolute obedience to parents and children working out the mutual honor, respect, and love modeled by the lifestyle of Jesus. This trajectory is taken for granted by most of us in virtually all of the above. If we are to speak for the dignity and equality of any one person, group, or class, we must speak out for all.

The Journey Toward Equal Relationships

The pilgrimage of life contains many journeys which parallel the three types of human relationship we have discussed here. In early childhood the child is complementary to the parents, in youth the symmetrical process of differentiation occurs, in maturity we stand parallel as fellow adults. So in marriage we fuse in the complementary attachment of our sexual and developmental uniqueness. Then in mid-marriage we work out in symmetrical differentiation and personal identity formation the full personhood of each. Then equal, mature adult relating becomes possible.

In stress we regress back to fighting and hassling or bickering and dickering in the old familiar symmetrical cycles. When these are recognized for what they are—"Hey, look, see what we're doing to each other, it's the old familiar dance"—they can be interrupted and negotiation to resolve tension and create more mutual parallel intimacy can be resumed.

A relationship is as mature as its covenant is equal, and both the maturity and the quality of our lives—yours and mine—are best measured by the quality of the relationships we are able to create with those we love.

Notes

1. George R. Bach and Peter Wyden, *The Intimate Enemy* (New York: Avon Books, 1968) pp. 159-163.
2. Donald Meichenbaum, *Cognitive-Behavior Modification* (New York: Plenum Press, 1977) pp. 94-95.
3. Manuel J. Smith, *When I Say No, I Feel Guilty* (New York: Bantam Books, Inc., 1975) p. 104.
4. David Johnson, *Reaching Out* (Englewood Cliffs: Prentice-Hall Inc., 1972) pp. 210-211.
5. Muriel Schiffman, *Gestalt Self Therapy* (Berkeley: Wingbow Press, 1971) pp. 77-84.
6. David Augsburger, *Caring Enough to Hear* (Ventura, CA: Regal Books, 1982) p. 113.
7. Murray Bowen, *Family Therapy in Clinical Practice* (New York: Jason Aaronson, Inc., 1978) pp. 145-146.
8. Mendel Lieberman and Marion Hardie, *Resolving Conflicts* (Santa Cruz: Unity Press, 1981) p. 111.
9. Sharon Bower and Gordon Bower, *Asserting Yourself* (Reading, MA: Addison-Wesley Publishing Co., 1976) p. 68.
10. George R. Bach and Peter Wyden, *The Intimate Enemy* (New York: Avon Books, 1968) pp. 80-82.
11. Frank Stagg, *Polarities of Man's Existence* (Philadelphia: Westminster Press, 1973) p. 161.
12. Don Jackson and William Lederer, *The Mirages of Marriage* (New York: W.W. Norton & Company, Inc., 1968) pp. 150-160.
13. John Scanzoni, *Love and Negotiate.* (Waco, TX: Word Books Inc., 1979) p. 16.

Bibliography

Augsburger, David. *Caring Enough to Confront.* Ventura: Regal Books, 1980.

______. *Caring Enough to Forgive/to Not Forgive.* Ventura: Regal Books, 1981.

______. *Caring Enough to Hear and Be Heard.* Ventura: Regal Books, 1982.

Bach, George and Goldberg, Herb. *Creative Aggression.* New York: Doubleday & Company, Inc., 1974.

Bach, George and Wyden, Peter. *The Intimate Enemy.* New York: Avon Books, 1968.

Bower, Sharon and Bower, Gordon. *Asserting Yourself.* Reading, MA: Addison-Wesley Publishing Co., 1976.

Faul, John and Augsburger, David. *Beyond Assertiveness.* Waco: Word Books Inc., 1979.

Fisher, Roger and Ury, William. *Getting to Yes.* Boston: Houghton Mifflin Co., 1981.

James, Muriel and Jongeward, Dorothy. *Born to Win.* Menlo Park: Addison-Wesley Publishing Company, Inc., 1971.

Lieberman, Mendel and Hardie, Marion. *Resolving Family Conflict.* Santa Cruz: Unity Press, 1981.

Miller, Sherod; Nunnally, Elam; Wackman, Daniel. *Alive and Aware.* Minneapolis: Interpersonal Communication Programs, 1975.

Powell, John. *Why Am I Afraid to Tell You Who I Am?* Niles, IL: Argus Communications, 1969.

Satir, Virginia. *Peoplemaking.* Palo Alto: Science and Behavior Books, Inc., 1972.

Scanzoni, John. *Love and Negotiate.* Waco: Word Books Inc., 1979.

Schiffman, Muriel. *Gestalt Self Therapy.* Berkley: Wingbow Press, 1971.